# GENERAL EDUCATION: Issues and Resources
Prepared by
The Project on General Education Models
Society for Values in Higher Education

## Authors

Jerry M. Chance
Clifton F. Conrad
Michael L. Davis
Jerry G. Gaff
John P. Nichols
Judith A. Redwine

## Editors

Jerry G. Gaff
Jack Lindquist
Kathryn Mohrman
Charles H. Reynolds
Rebecca Yount

Published by the Association of American Colleges

# Contents

# About the Authors and Editors

**Jerry M. Chance** (Th.D.) is Associate Professor and Chairman of the Department of Philosophy and Religion at Florida Agricultural and Mechanical University. He teaches courses in Religion and Literature, Contemporary Religious Thought, and Aesthetics; has received grants from the Florida Endowment for the Humanities and the Florida Bicentennial Commission; and is a member of the Editorial Committee of the Center for the Study of Southern Culture and Religion at Florida State University.

**Clifton F. Conrad** is Associate Professor of Higher Education at The College of William and Mary in Virginia; he has a doctorate in higher education from the University of Michigan, and has taught at the University of Denver and Indiana University. His most recent book is *The Undergraduate Curriculum: A Guide to Innovation and Reform* (Westview, 1978), and he is currently finishing a monograph on liberal education for the American Association for Higher Education and the EIRC Clearinghouse on Higher Education.

**Michael L. Davis** is Assistant to the Academic Vice President at the University of the Pacific. He holds a Ph.D. in experimental psychology from the University of Utah; he coordinates faculty development and curriculum development activities on the UOP campus. His interest in evaluation grows out of his background in experimental psychology and centers on educational programs.

**Jerry G. Gaff** is Director of the Project on General Education Models. After earning a doctorate in social psychology from Syracuse University, he taught both sociology and psychology. At the University of California, Berkeley, he conducted research and authored books on experimental colleges, faculty impact on students, and faculty development. Recently he has directed action projects aimed at improving the quality of undergraduate education.

**Jack Lindquist** serves as Director of the Institute for Academic Improvement at Memphis State University. His most recent book is *Increasing the Impact* (Council for the Advancement of Small Colleges, 1980). Since obtaining his Ph.D. from the University of Michigan, he has been actively involved with institutional change strategies and the improvement of undergraduate education. He is particularly interested in the intellectual and ethical development of students.

**Kathryn Mohrman** is editor of *The Forum for Liberal Education* and director of the Office of National Affairs at the Association of American Colleges. Educated at Grinnell College, the University of Wisconsin, and George Washington University, she has spoken and written about general education curricula, innovations in humanities teaching, and funding for academic programs. She has a special interest in policies for education and training for adult learners.

**John P. Nichols** earned advanced degrees in theology (S.T.L., Fribourg, Switzerland) and in philosophy (Ph.D., Louvain, Belgium) and acquired a strong commitment to interdisciplinary studies and methodology in the process. He currently holds the rank of Professor of Philosophy and is Coordinator of the Core Curriculum at Saint Joseph's College in Indiana. In June of 1979, he directed a group of Saint Joseph's faculty in a five-day institute on "Designing a Core Curriculum," an Institute attended by eighty faculty from other colleges and funded by a Project Grant from the National Endowment for the Humanities. Dr. Nichols is engaged in faculty development work in the areas of interdisciplinary skills and integrated student skills development.

**Judith A. Redwine** is Acting Director of Extended Programs at Indiana University at South Bend, a position which enables her to coordinate all off-campus and external degree studies. She holds a Ph.D. in educational administration and supervision from the University of Notre Dame. She has special interests in adult students, innovative instructional delivery systems, faculty development, curriculum development, and teaching improvement and evaluation.

**Charles H. Reynolds** is Associate Professor of Religious Studies at the University of Tennessee-Knoxville. He obtained a Ph.D. from Harvard University and is currently teaching religious ethics, bioethics, and legal philosophy. He is the editor of *The Journal of Religious Ethics.* Dr. Reynolds has a long-range interest in general education and is presently involved in a broad-based curriculum review on the Knoxville campus.

**Rebecca Yount** is Assistant to the Director, Project on General Education Models. She was educated at Capital University, SUNY-Binghamton, and New York University. Her past publications include *Political Handbook of the World* (McGraw-Hill, 1975 and 1976), and she edited the *PIRIT Newsletter* that was issued by the Project on Institutional Renewal for the Improvement of Teaching. Currently she is editor of the *GEM Newsletter*, a Project GEM publication which addresses issues in general education.

# 1. Introduction

It is no longer news that general education is in disarray. Over two years have elapsed since the Carnegie Foundation for the Advancement of Teaching declared that "general education is a disaster area," and since the faculty at Harvard University began debating the report of its Task Force on the Core Curriculum. It is also no longer news that these two highly publicized events touched off what has been called a "new national debate about general education," as countless individuals in the nation's colleges and universities have voiced their concerns about the quality of undergraduate general education.

What *is* new is that the debate has turned into action. Conferences have been held to discuss the issues; articles and books have been published to expound analyses and proposals; projects have been initiated to understand and solve some of the problems; educational associations have mounted new programs to support curricular reform; and foundations have begun to fund changes in the curriculum. Above all, hundreds of colleges and universities have taken concrete steps to strengthen their general education programs. Today many committees, task forces, or ad hoc groups at a wide variety of institutions are reviewing their general education programs and attempting to forge improvements.

This marks the first time since the days immediately following World War II that sustained national attention has been directed toward general education. Because the world is radically different now, it is necessary to think about general education in fresh ways. This effort stands in marked contrast to the last wave of curricular reform in the 1960's when, fired by slogans urging individuals to "do their own thing," school after school relaxed or dropped requirements. Today's challenge is to reconstruct general education, a vastly more difficult and complex endeavor than simply removing restrictions. These circumstances call for creativity in designing general education for the contemporary context.

In what directions are curricular reforms moving? At first blush it appears that reformers are marching off in all directions. Although many have been swayed by calls for a core curriculum, some interpret this as meaning a

1

common body of knowledge for their students; others stress common skills and abilities; others seek common experiences, not exclusively curricular, as a means to rebuild the academic community; and still others see little reason to require anything common to all students.

Amid the conflicting analyses and proposals, two schools of thought and action stand out. One stresses the reinstitution of conventional distribution requirements, which consist primarily of traditional academic disciplines, usually taught with familiar lecture and seminar methods. Proponents tend to accept the rhetoric of "back to basics" and to believe that more structure is necessary to improve the quality of education. They harken back to the golden days before the curriculum was loosened by the concern for relevance, and before the preference for career education led students away from the liberal arts.

There are two serious limitations to this approach. First, an array of disciplinary offerings with a specified pattern of distribution requirements is the one model of general education with which we have had extensive experience recently, and many of the problems we face today attest to its limitations: the fragmented character of the curriculum, the absence of an accepted philosophy or rationale, lack of student interest, loss of faculty commitment, and no centralized coordination or administration of general education. Furthermore, breadth is only one part of what most people accept as components of general education. Basic and advanced learning skills, integrative learning, and exploration of value implications of knowledge are additional components, which are usually not addressed by distribution requirements.

The second school of thought resists the all too human tendency to return to familiar patterns. While agreeing that the integrity of general education needs to be re-established, proponents argue that new models need to be devised which will be appropriate to our times. The approach of developing new curricula is laborious and it does not hold out the promise of success, simply because those who choose this course must sail in uncharted waters. It demands a great deal of innovative thinking and acting precisely at a time when campus morale and fiscal flexibility have sunk to low levels. But it does represent the best opportunity to reconstruct this vital portion of undergraduate education.

In this endeavor to reconstruct the curriculum, each college or university must devise a program appropriate to its own circumstances. That is, it must be consistent with the mission, history and character of the institution; to the needs and interests of its students; and to the talents and interests of its faculty.

The improvement of general education is a complex undertaking. It includes many different elements, such as the curriculum, instruction, advisement, and evaluation. It requires the understanding and support of many different people and interest groups, including students, faculty members, and administrators—sometimes even boards of trustees, state officials, employers, and citizens. Furthermore, it involves intellectual components, since it requires knowledge of how best to produce the qualities desired in students, as well as political components, because any change requires the approval of a great many interest groups.

This volume has been prepared to assist individuals and groups as they review general education at their own institutions and seek to fashion more effective programs. This compilation of ideas, programs, and people is intended to provide information, broaden perspectives about what can be done, and help to highlight strengths and weaknesses of several alternative approaches.

The topics included in this guide grew out of the practical needs of faculty members and administrators who are providing leadership for the revision of general education at institutions participating in the Project on General Education Models. One of the first requests made by participants in this national project was for information about useful resources. Conversations with these individuals, as well as among an editorial group that was assembled to direct this effort, revealed that the interests coalesced around the major topics that form the several chapters of this volume: historical and contemporary perspectives of general education; students and objectives; curricular approaches; non-curricular dimensions; teaching and advising; strategies for implementing changes; and evaluation. There is inevitable overlap among the chapters, since these topics are not mutually exclusive; indeed, they are all systemically related to one another.

Most chapters include four sections. First is a short essay that offers perspectives, draws pertinent distinctions, raises some key isues, identifies major trends, or points to some of the current controversies in the area. There are a variety of points of view represented in the essays, since they are written by different authors. These are not intended as definitive statements, but they are designed to be thought-provoking as well as to assist the actual process of change.

The second part is an annotated bibliography. Obviously, each chapter can include only a small portion of the published literature; the items included are highly selective, and some resources have been omitted because of lack of space. A few principles of selection have been followed. Wide coverage of each topic has been sought by including only a few items on any of the several subtopics in each chapter and by limiting the number of listings of any one author. The most basic references, those judged to render a cogent treatment of some significant portion of the topic, have been given preference over less cogent ones. Works with practical implications have been favored over those that are merely intellectually interesting. Items that are readily available on college campuses have been included rather than fugitive documents that may be hard to locate or expensive to acquire. Recent material has been stressed rather than older so as to reflect better the contemporary realities in higher education. Preference also has been given to writings that avoid jargon, sophisticated methodology, and complex statistical analyses. A more extensive listing of additional bibliographic material, the third part of each chapter, helps to increase the number and range of entries that are cited.

The fourth section consists of a list of programs, organizations, and individuals who direct them. Often it is more important to know that a certain type of program actually exists, or the name of someone who can be contacted for information about why it was established and how it actually operates, than it is to read an article analyzing the issues. The people involved in innovative programs have experience (often acquired the hard way) that can be instructive to those interested in embarking on similar improvements. A few illustrative programs in each topic, therefore, are included.

If individuals approach this volume with the mindset of shopping for specific curricular models which they might adopt or of looking for clear-cut answers to the many questions surrounding general education, they will be disappointed. The state of the art does not permit such certainty, and the appropriation of a holistic model from another institution is almost always a fatal course of action. This book rather, is intended to articulate many of the issues that are involved in the revision of general education and to guide the reader to some resources that may be useful in shaping new programs. In keeping with these interests, this volume is purposefully eclectic and avoids being prescriptive.

The impetus for the preparation of this guidebook came from the Project on General Education Models (GEM). Sponsored by the Society for Values in Higher Education, Project GEM is a temporary consortium of 13 colleges and universities. The institutions include: Bucknell University, Lewisburg, Pennsylvania; Carroll College, Waukesha, Wisconsin; Catonsville Community College, Catonsville, Maryland; Community College of Denver, Colorado; Florida Agricultural and Mechanical University, Tallahassee, Florida; Indiana University at South Bend, Indiana; Northeastern Illinois University, Chicago, Illinois; Oregon State University, Corvallis, Oregon; Rochester Institute of Technology (including both the College of General Studies and the National Technical Institute for the Deaf), Rochester, New York; State University of New York College at Brockport, Brockport, New York; University of the Pacific, Stockton, California; and Valparaiso University, Valparaiso, Indiana. The Project is a three-year organization supported by grants from the Exxon Education Foundation and the Fund for the Improvement of Postsecondary Education, U.S. Department of Health, Education and Welfare. Each participating institution has appointed a task force consisting of faculty members, students, and administrators, all of whom combine to provide leadership for the reform of general education. This volume was prepared originally as a way to give the individuals associated with the Project access to useful resources that could inform and enhance their work.

The Society for Values in Higher Education has an active membership of approximately 1,500 individuals representing all academic disciplines. Located in New Haven, Connecticut, the Society traces its beginnings as far back as 1923 and the efforts of the distinguished Yale scholar, Charles Kent, to encourage teaching and scholarship in higher education. Among the many important functions of the Society has been sponsorship of projects, such as GEM, related to the improvement of higher education.

The Association of American Colleges is a national organization concerned with promoting liberal and humane education and with strengthening the institutions that provide it. Since general education is seen as a central component of liberal education, the Association collaborated in the preparation of this document. By publishing this manuscript, the Association is able to make it available not only to its members, but to all those interested in the reconstruction of general education.

Many individuals played a vital role in the preparation of this volume. The editorial group was assembled to plan the general character of the monograph. Then individual authors were solicited to write specific chapters; most of them are faculty members with interests in a particular area of general education. Their drafts were reviewed by the editorial group to ensure that each contained useful and current material, that there was reasonable consistency among the sections in terms of length, style, and tone, and that overlaps were minimized. In short, this has been a collaborative effort that, in many respects, mirrors the very task of designing a coherent general education program.

The contributions of several other individuals to the preparation of this volume deserve special acknowledgement. Judith deSerio of the American Council on Education Library provided assistance and advice about publications. Lynn Haupt at the ERIC Clearinghouse on Higher Education operated by George Washington University conducted a literature search that proved very useful. Charles Bunting, Richard Hendrix, and Carol Stoel of the Fund for the Improvement of Postsecondary Education shared their knowledge of programs and organizations that could serve as resources for others. John Hager of the Association of American Colleges helped to assemble information about resource programs and projects. Helpful critiques of an early version of the manuscript were provided by Arthur Levine of the Carnegie Council on Policy Studies for Higher Education, Jeffrey Lukenbill of Miami-Dade Community College, Dean Whitla of Harvard University, and Curtis Huber of Pacific Lutheran University. A thorough critique of a later draft was made by Sally Gaff. A careful proofreading of the manuscript was done by David Yount. The preliminary draft was typed by Dolly Angelette, and later versions by David Gaff, Jane Holcomb, and Diane Haddick.

# 2.  General Resources

To be successful in curricular revision, academic professionals must be knowledgeable about the whole of higher education and about current developments concerning general education in particular. Faculty members typically are knowledgeable about their academic disciplines but often are not as aware of curricular and related developments in higher education. Administrators similarly may lack a detailed understanding of important developments at other institutions and the sense of how they may be of use at their own schools. Given these limitations, it should be no surprise that, as one person commented wryly, curriculum proposals tend to be auto-biographical—that is, they reflect the necessarily limited personal experience and views of individuals involved. The resources given here have been prepared as a guide to the many information sources about higher education so that they can expand and enrich the work of those planning and implementing curricular revisions.

Materials contained in this chapter are general in two senses. Some deal generally with higher education issues and help to place the current activity concerning general education within a broad context. Such is the case with the periodicals, journals, publishers, newsletters, and other publications that are listed. Some other information sources deal with several aspects of general education and are not able to be categorized as belonging within any one of the separate chapters. They are general in that they are relevant to a large number of topics concerning the revision of general education. These items include centers for the study of higher education, organizations and special projects that focus on general education, and several basic readings on general education.

These materials can help individuals who find themselves on a curriculum committee charged with the task of proposing revisions in the general education program with the means to overcome parochial perspectives and familiar ways of doing things. As such, these persons may be able to prepare sounder proposals or develop more effective programs than would otherwise be possible.

## A. PERIODICALS

There are two major general publications containing essential, timely, readable material about all facets of higher education:

*The Chronicle of Higher Education* is a specialized newspaper containing articles on current events in higher education. It also includes a list of newly published books, notifications of job changes, book reviews, a calendar of future events, and an extensive listing of job openings. Weekly. $25 per year. 1333 New Hampshire Avenue, N.W., Washington, D.C. 20036.

*Change Magazine* presents a wide variety of thoughtful articles on various aspects of higher education as well as reports on major Washington developments affecting colleges and universities. It offers summaries of research projects, extended reviews of books, and reports from individual campuses. Monthly. $18 per year. NBW Tower, New Rochelle, New York 10801.

## B. JOURNALS

Scholarly journals remain the primary vehicle for communicating information about higher education. There are many journals that carry informative articles related to general education. Some of the most useful and most accessible non-technical publications are listed below:

*Alternative Higher Education* is a journal of nontraditional studies. It features articles on experiential learning, individualized studies, lifelong learning, and alternative programs and courses. Quarterly. $15 per year. Human Sciences Press, 72 Fifth Avenue, New York, New York 10011.

*American Educational Research Journal* publishes original research on all levels of education, but nearly every issue contains some articles related to higher education. Quarterly. $14 per year. American Educational Research Association, 1126 16th Street, N.W., Washington, D.C. 20036.

*Educational Record* contains several articles in each edition that assess contemporary issues. The articles are fairly short but cover a wide range of topics. Quarterly. $15 per year. American Council on Education, One Dupont Circle, N.W., Washington, D.C. 20036.

*Harvard Educational Review* tends to emphasize various themes or issues. The articles traverse all levels of education, and they are thoughtful and thorough. Quarterly. $16 per year. Business Office, Harvard University, Longfellow Hall, 13 Appian Way, Cambridge, Massachusetts 02138.

*Improving College and University Teaching* features brief items on teaching written by faculty. Although the articles are too short to offer more than a superficial discussion of the topic, the variety of issues touched upon can be stimulating. Quarterly. $12 per year. Oregon State University Press, 101 Waldo Hall, Oregon State University, Corvallis, Oregon 97331.

*Journal of General Education* publishes various types of articles, including historical perspectives, institutional case studies, humanistic critiques, and pleas for reforms. Quarterly. $12 per year. Pennsylvania State University Press, 215 Wagner Building, University Park, Pennsylvania 16802.

*Journal of Higher Education* contains thoughtful analyses and criticisms of new approaches to education. Some articles emphasize curricular and instructional matters, while others focus on governance and management practices. Bimonthly. $14 per year. Ohio State University Press, 2070 Neil Avenue, Columbus, Ohio 43210.

*Liberal Education* features articles that relate primarily to the liberal arts and sciences and to all institutions that support liberal learning, including two- and four-year colleges and universities as well as graduate and professional schools. Quarterly. $9 per year. Association of American Colleges, 1818 R Street, N.W., Washington, D.C. 20009.

*Research in Higher Education* presents research reports on various aspects of higher education, some of which are related to general education. Monthly. $28 per year. APS Publications. Fulfillment Department. 49 Sheridan Avenue, Albany, New York 12210.

*Teachers College Record* publishes articles across the broad spectrum of education. Quarterly. $14 per year. Teachers College, Columbia University, 525 West 120th Street, New York, New York 10027.

In addition to these comprehensive journals, there are also many more specialized publications which feature topical articles in general education. These and their particular emphases include: *Higher Education*, international perspectives and reports; *Journal of Educational Psychology*, psychological and educational studies; *Review of Educational Research*, reviews of research in various areas; and *Sociology of Education*, sociological studies.

Furthermore, many of the professional societies in specific disciplines publish journals related to the improvement of instruction in their fields. In some cases the entire publication is directed toward this effort; in the majority of cases a few sections or features deal with pedagogical issues, while the bulk of the journal is devoted to expository articles about the subject itself. A sampling of associations and their publications includes: American Chemical Society, *Journal of Chemical Education*; Council on Anthropology and Education, *Anthropology and Education Quarterly*; American Political Science Association, *NEWS for Teachers of Political Science* (formerly *DEA News*), a quarterly newspaper; American Society for Engineering Education, *Engineering Education*; National Council of Teachers of English, *English Education*, *College English*, and *College Composition and Communication*; Mathematical Association of America, *American Mathematical Monthly* and *Two-Year College Mathematics Journal*. For additional journals, faculty can check directly with their disciplinary associations.

## C. BOOK PUBLISHERS

Although many publishers offer books on higher education, the following two have the most comprehensive lists in terms of general education:

*Jossey-Bass, Inc., Publishers*, has the most extensive list of books on virtually all facets of the field. It sells almost exclusively by mail, although a selection is available in almost all college and university libraries. Jossey-Bass also publishes the reports of the Carnegie Council on Policy Studies, consisting of major statements of a topical nature on national issues in American higher education. 433 California Street, San Francisco, California 94104.

*Change Magazine Press* publishes a rapidly growing roster of books on a wide variety of academic areas, including major book essays on key issues of curriculum, learning, the state of academic science research, and an extended series of books designed to serve the special needs of academic professionals. NBW Tower, New Rochelle, New York 10801.

## D. NEWSLETTERS

Newsletters are excellent vehicles for finding out about many issues affecting general education. Some are free; others are available at modest cost. They include the following:

*AAHE Bulletin*, published by the American Association for Higher Education, includes the Research Currents series of four-page reports that summarize research on topics of current concern. Ten times yearly. $20 (free to AAHE members). American Association for Higher Education, One Dupont Circle, N.W., Washington, D.C. 20036.

*Alternatives* is the voice of the Resource Center for Planned Change, an arm of the American Association of State Colleges and Universities. It presents essays on topics of concern in higher education, reports of seminars and task force meetings with its Center Associates, and describes innovations in such areas as faculty development, program evaluation, programs for new clienteles, and academic planning. Two to four times yearly. $4. Resource Center for Planned Change, American Association of State Colleges and Universities, One Dupont Circle, N.W., Washington, D.C. 20036.

*Faculty Development and Evaluation in Higher Education* has a wealth of information including descriptions of campus programs, original articles on issues related to its areas of focus, a list of new publications in these areas, and book reviews. It is becoming a major communication mechanism among practitioners of faculty development and evaluation. Quarterly. $5 per year. Faculty Development and Evaluation, University of Florida, 340 Norman Hall, Gainsville, Florida 32611.

*Findings* highlights research conducted by the Educational Testing Service by presenting focused, easy-to-read articles growing out of the various topics it researches. Implications for educational practice are usually discussed. Quarterly. Free. Educational Testing Service, Princeton, New Jersey 08540.

*Forum for Liberal Education* is a topic-oriented publication featuring a subject of importance for liberal education in each issue. Recent issues include discussions of the core curriculum, general education, and student outcomes. Each issue typically contains an article dealing with issues, various campus program descriptions, and a list of useful resources. Bimonthly. $18 per year. Association of American Colleges, 1818 R Street, N.W., Washington, D.C. 20009.

*GEM Newsletter* is a publication of the Project on General Education Models. Each issue highlights a topic of concern to general education, reports on activities at certain of the 13 member institutions, and information about additional resources. 8-10 issues during the three years of the Project. $12.50 for the series. Project on General Education Models, 1818 R Street, N.W., Washington, D.C. 20009.

*HERI Quarterly* contains brief notes concerning research activities and some findings of its various studies. Quarterly. Free. Higher Education Research Institute, 924 Westwood Boulevard, Los Angeles, California 90024.

*Higher Education and National Affairs* features information about federal policies affecting higher education as well as notices of important developments throughout the country. Multiple copies are distributed to each member institution of the American Council on Education; since this includes most schools, copies should be readily available on many campuses. Weekly. Free to institutional members. American Council on Education, One Dupont Circle, N.W., Washington, D.C. 20009.

*Memo to the Faculty* consists of six-page reports that develop a particular theme appropriate to the problems, issues, and activities at the University of Michigan. Some recent themes include: Learning How to Learn Independently; The Extended Classroom; Grading by Contract; Student Reactions to Instruction; and Service and Research for Teachers. Back issues on a variety of teaching and learning topics are available on request. Quarterly. $2 per year. Center for Research on Learning and Teaching, University of Michigan, 109 East Madison, Ann Arbor, Michigan 48104.

*Memo to the President* has current topics of interest to presidents of state colleges and universities, such as federal affairs, important news items, upcoming conferences, and educational trends. Biweekly. $7 per year. American Association of State Colleges and Universities, One Dupont Circle, Washington, D.C. 20036.

*Newsletter of the Council of Colleges of Arts and Sciences* features timely items about activities in federal agencies and professional associations of interest to deans of liberal arts colleges in public universities. Quarterly. Free. Council of Colleges of Arts and Sciences. One Dupont Circle, Washington, D.C. 20036.

*Teaching-Learning Issues* discusses topics related to teaching and learning with emphasis on available research. The literature is well summarized, and each issue focuses on a certain topic, such as interdisciplinary instruction, the Keller Plan, and other topics. Three times a year. Free. Learning Research Center, University of Tennessee, Knoxville, Tennessee 37916.

## E. OTHER PUBLICATIONS

A few special focus publications contain information of value to general education curriculum planners.

Educational Resources Information Center (ERIC)
Clearinghouse on Higher Education
George Washington University
Washington, D.C. 20036
Jonathan D. Fife, Director
This is a clearinghouse of publications. It collects, files, and provides access to extensive number of publications that span the range of topics and institutions of higher education. Several reports are available on various topics, and individualized literature searches are possible on specified topics.

Educational Resources Information Center (ERIC)
Clearinghouse on Junior Colleges
University of California, Los Angeles, California 90024
Arthur M. Cohen, Director
Like the ERIC Clearinghouse above except that the focus is on the literature specifically relevant to community and junior colleges.

*AAHE-ERIC/Higher Education Research Reports* is a series of booklets or monographs that summarize research conducted on various topics. These are short, readable treatments with useful bibliographies. Examples of topics covered recently are curriculum development and evaluation, student learning styles, and interdisciplinary education. Ten per year. $4 for each issue. American Association for Higher Education, One Dupont Circle, N.W., Washington, D.C. 20036.

*New Directions* is the name of a series of several different journals, each with a different focus. *New Directions for Higher Education* is the most wide-ranging; other more specialized topics are community colleges, experiential learning, education and work, institutional advancement, institutional research, program evaluation, and student services. Each series is published quarterly. $15 per year for individuals; $25 for institutions. Jossey-Bass, Inc., Publishers, 433 California Street, San Francisco, California 94104.

*Reports on Teaching* is a special series of six reports that describe effective undergraduate teaching that has been identified within major scholarly fields. Areas covered in depth include: chemistry, psychology, history, English, biology, political science, mathematics, philosophy, languages, and interdisciplinary study. These have been widely circulated and should be available on most campuses. $1 for each Report. *Change Magazine*, NBW Tower, New Rochelle, New York 10801.

*Resources for Change: A Guide to Projects 1979-80* is an annual fall publication containing a one-page summary of all projects supported by the Fund for the Improvement of Postsecondary Education, U.S. Department of Health, Education, and Welfare. A wide range of projects that represent promising educational ventures is described. $3.25. Superintendent of Documents, U.S. Government Printing Office, Washington, D.C. 20402.

## F. CENTERS FOR THE STUDY OF HIGHER EDUCATION

Several centers have been established to study higher education, provide graduate training for persons in the administration of higher education, and serve institutions in their regions. Staff members are knowledgeable about higher education in general, and some usually specialize in curriculum and instruction. A few of the more comprehensive and service-oriented ones are listed below:

Pennsylvania State University
University Park, Pennsylvania 16802
Center for the Study of Higher Education
Kenneth P. Mortimer, Director

State University of New York
Buffalo, New York 14214
Department of Higher Education
Robert O. Berdahl, Chairman

University of California
Los Angeles, California 90024
Higher Education Specialization Program
Graduate School of Education
Frederick C. Kintzer, Head

University of Georgia
Athens, Georgia 30602
Institute of Higher Education
Cameron Fincher, Director

University of Michigan
Ann Arbor, Michigan 48104
Center for the Study of Higher Education
Marvin W. Peterson, Director

University of Texas
Austin, Texas 78712
Program in Community College Education
School of Education
John E. Roueche, Chairman

## G. ORGANIZATIONS AND SPECIAL PROJECTS

A number of special projects, programs, or services dealing with general education have been established in recent years. They are supported by such diverse groups as national academic associations, professional societies, state systems, and consortia. Staff members at these organizations often are at the heart of information networks, and they can put individuals in touch with others to discuss their ideas or concerns. Some staff members also may take time to share their experiences or react to specific inquiries. Frequently, it is possible to purchase materials or to be placed on a mailing list to receive periodic reports or newsletters. A few such organizations are:

Association for General and Liberal Studies
Carol J. Guardo, President
Dean of Liberal Arts
Drake University
Des Moines, Iowa 50311
The Association is an individual membership organization devoted primarily to undergraduate general and liberal education. It holds an annual conference where ideas are explored, innovative approaches are examined, and undergraduate education improvement is promoted.

Association of American Colleges
Mark H. Curtis, President
1818 R Street, N.W.
Washington, D.C. 20009
Serving a membership of colleges and universities, the Association provides a range of services designed to promote liberal learning at the member institutions. In addition to its annual meeting, it offers workshops for academic deans and department chairpersons, advisory services to evaluate and improve liberal learning among its members, and information about federal funding programs. It also issues an array of publications, including *Liberal Education*, *Forum for Liberal Education*, and *TRENDS 2000*. Special projects focus on the status and education of women, faculty development, and presidential selection services.

College Outcome Measures Project
Aubrey Forrest, Director
American College Testing Program
Iowa City, Iowa 52242
This is a special project to design, develop, validate, and implement assessment instruments and procedures to measure and evaluate the knowledge, skills, and attitudes acquired by undergraduate students. Of greatest concern are those outcomes resulting from general or liberal education programs or those relevant to effective functioning in adult roles. The instruments and procedures are being pilot-tested in a group of participating institutions, and the research results and assessment materials will be made available for wider use.

Council for the Advancement of Small Colleges
Gary H. Quehl, President
One Dupont Circle, N.W.
Washington, D.C. 20036
This organization has pioneered new approaches to faculty, administrative, and curriculum development, and has helped to establish operational programs in its member institutions. It publishes a small but useful list of

books, operates a low-cost national consulting service, and has a wealth of experience in fostering institution-wide educational improvements.

General Education Study
Leonard Bowman, Director
University House
University of Iowa
Iowa City, Iowa 52242
In 1978 faculty from five small, independent colleges met for the purpose of learn ng more about the general education component of the curriculum. Eact of their respective institutions is involved in reviewing or reconstructing its curriculum. This study has helped each to determine ways by which to improve its general education program, and is entitled *Five Colleges Look at General Education* (ERIC ED168 434).

National Project IV: Examining the Varieties of Liberal Education
Zelda Gamson, Director
Center for the Study of Higher Education 2007 SEB
University of Michigan
Ann Arbor, Michigan 48109
This project consists of a group of diverse postsecondary institutions undertaking an assessment and dissemination of their different models of liberal education. Collaboration among the associate institutions will result in publication about liberal learning and ways to strengthen it.

Project on General Education Models
Jerry G. Gaff, Director
1818 R Street, N.W.
Washington, D.C. 20009
This Project involves a group of 13 diverse colleges and universities, each of which is seeking to reconstruct its general education program. A small central staff assisted by an advisory board prepares materials, holds workships and conferences, and convenes meetings of representatives to assist the work of each institutional task force. The *GEM Newsletter*, faculty interview form, and student questionnaire are available. The progress of the work at each campus as well as the outcomes and materials from the project as a whole can be followed by subscribers to the newsletter.

Shakertown Conference
Thomas Maher, Convener
Professional Development Center
Wichita State University
Wichita, Kansas 67208
A series of conversations on general/liberal education is held at Shakertown, Kentucky annually. Participation is by invitation. Philosophical issues and practical considerations are examined by faculty members and administrators during the course of the event.

Small College Consortium
2000 P Street, N.W.
Suite 400
Washington, D.C. 20036
Thomas H. Englund, Executive Director
Comprehensive institutional development is the goal of this group of 51 colleges. Assistance with curriculum development, faculty development and evaluation, administrator development and evaluation, student recruitment and retention, planning and management practices, and career and student development are provided to the schools. This is a Title III Consortium.


## H. BASIC READINGS

Much has been written about the many facets of general education, but a few volumes appear repeatedly on lists of references. Some of the more widely influential recent books are listed below:

Boyer, E. and Kaplan, M. *Educating for Survival*, New Rochelle, N.Y.: Change Magazine Press, 1977.
> Authors assert that ". . . social survival in this and the next century is more likely when a common sharing of our human voyage is rediscovered by our educational leaders. A core curriculum can be built around a few clusters of ideas and events that influenced our past, key issues that affect our present lives, some images and alternatives for the future, and the formulation of values and personal beliefs." Several suggestions of organizing principles are offered.

Carnegie Foundation for the Advancement of Teaching, *Missions of the College Curriculum*, San Francisco: Jossey-Bass, 1977.
> A comprehensive treatment of the curriculum. Discusses factors that influence the curriculum, relationship of education to work and to society, and evaluation of effectiveness. Treats several aspects of the curriculum, including the core, major, electives, and general education. Suggests directions for updating and reforming courses of study.

Chickering, A. *Education and Identity*. San Francisco: Jossey-Bass, 1969.
> A synthesis of research on student development organized around a theory of personality development. Author identifies several college conditions that influence the general education of students. A well written book that contains practical steps which a college can take to promote student growth.

Chickering, A., Halliburton, D., Bergquist, W., and Lindquist, J. *Curriculum: A Handbook for Faculty and Administrators*, Washington, D.C.: Council for the Advancement of Small Colleges, 1977.
> Focuses on four major aspects of curriculum: rationale (Chickering); design (Halliburton); practices (Bergquist); and implementation (Lindquist). Includes chapters on major social changes, obstacles to curriculum development, determining objectives, and formulation and decision making, as well as implementation and evaluation of curricular reform. Eight models are explained, specific college examples given, and curricular planning tools offered.

Cross, K. *Accent on Learning*. San Francisco: Jossey-Bass, 1976.
> A lucid discussion of which instructional approaches work best for the "new" students who have enrolled in colleges as a result of open admissions policies. Some of the more important suggestions concern student development outside the curriculum — education for personal development, learning about people from people, and interpersonal skills.

Grant, G. and Riesman, D. *The Perpetual Dream: Reform and Experiment in the American College*. Chicago: University of Chicago Press, 1978.
> Educational dreams of both visionaries and pragmatists took form in large numbers of experiments during the 1960's, "as volatile a period of educational reform as America has ever experienced." Based on hundreds of interviews with faculty and students, this work

studies reforms, both telic (which redefine goals) and popular (which are initiated in response to specific social and political developments). Vignettes of innovative institutions are included.

Levine, A. *Handbook on Undergraduate Curriculum*. San Francisco: Jossey-Bass, 1978.
This is a comprehensive treatment of many curricular aspects — general education, the major, basic and advanced skills, tests and grades, education and work, advising, credits and degrees, methods of instruction, and structure of academic time. A rich source of ideas about leading educators, distinctive curricula, history of curriculum change, and cross-cultural comparisons.

Rudolph, F. *Curriculum: A History of the American Undergraduate Course of Study Since 1636*. San Francisco: Jossey-Bass, 1977.
An excellent analysis of the curriculum from colonial times to the present. The curriculum is viewed as an instrument of many purposes and persons, both internal and external to an institution. Major themes in the curriculum and curricular change are discussed.

# 3. Historical and Contemporary Perspectives

## By Jerry G. Gaff

General education is a timeless concern. Thinkers and writers in various ages and cultures have voiced ideals for individuals and societies that undergird current concepts of general education. The ancient Greeks, for example, regarded education not just as an individual pursuit but as a communal activity "...by which a community preserves and transmits its physical and intellectual character" (Jaeger, 1945, p. xiii). In such a context, it is understandable that educated individuals were expected to provide leadership for the state, and according to Jaeger, "The Greek trinity of poet, statesman, and sage embodied the nation's highest ideal of leadership" (p. xxvi). The warrior, athlete, artist, priest, scientist, and scholar have been idealized in other times, and shaped by both formal and informal education.

The pursuit of each of these ideals requires different, often specialized, skills. Sometimes the requisite education is provided in special purpose institutions such as the military academy. Other times it occurs in various parts of the same institution, as within the comprehensive university. In any case, students are taught to attend to certain aspects of the world, think in a limited number of categories, adopt prevailing values for that particular ideal, and embark on a preferred pathway through life. The full realization of any one of these ideals may require a lifetime of experience to perfect, during which one progressively hones skills, encounters a range of practical experiences, and learns to deal with a level of complexity not recognized previously. Such practices are the hallmarks of specialization in education and work.

Yet there are commonalities. Each culture has an image of what a generally educated person is, regardless of specialty. For instance, he[1] typically is expected to be sophisticated in the use of language, to be widely knowledgeable about the society, and to have a sense of its history. Further-

---

[1]For stylistic purposes we have employed *he* rather than variations of he/she or him/her generically with the explicit understanding that this is not a reference to gender.

more, there are commonalities in the education of students regardless of specialty. In ancient and medieval universities all students were instructed in the *quadrivium* (arithmetic, geometry, astronomy, music) and the *trivium* (logic, grammar, rhetoric). Such practices were the precursors to contemporary programs of general education that involve a core curriculum, e.g., a common set of courses required of all students.

Throughout the history of American higher education, according to a recent author* (Rudolph, 1977, p. 3), "...change in the course of study has been constant, conscious and unconscious, gradual and sudden, accidental and intentional, uneven and diverse, imaginative and pedestrian." One of the dynamics has been the swing of the pendulum between the relative emphasis on specialized and general education (although there is not necessarily a contradiction between the two). Among those who have helped shape current views of general education are four persons who represent different views and times—John Henry Cardinal Newman writing in 1873, Alfred North Whitehead (1929), Robert Maynard Hutchins (1936), and Clark Kerr (1964).

Newman (1873) articulates an idealized vision of the university. Its purpose is defined simply as a setting for teaching and learning. Research is not an appropriate function, and he would have been appalled at recent proposals to use the university as a remedy for social ills, whether for liberal or conservative purposes. The context within which teaching and learning ought to occur is a community of scholars; current practices of awarding credit for prior experience and testing for competencies that permit individuals to avoid participation in this kind of community would be anathema. The goal for Newman is a liberal education, without direct practical or vocational applications, but one which prepares individuals for all of life. Humanistic study, especially of religion and literature, rather than science, is the best vehicle to this end. These categories have become conventional wisdom within many liberal arts circles.

Whitehead, a mathematician and philosopher, differs in many ways from Newman. He sees no essential difference between the study of the general culture and specialized knowledge; all are viewed as parts of the "seamless coat of learning." Further, he regards education as something useful. One of the surest ways to determine the effectiveness of education is whether ideas are connected with life; those that are not he labels "inert ideas." He argues that general education should be concerned with the concrete present; the primary value of the past is to equip one to deal effectively with one's present and future life. Whitehead's ideas, along with those of John Dewey and others, have contributed to the progressive spirit that inspired so much of higher education, including the establishment of "experimental" colleges during the 1920's and '30's, such as Bard, Bennington, and Sarah Lawrence.

The person perhaps most identified with general education in this country has been Hutchins. In terms of ideals and inclinations he is closer to Newman than to Whitehead. He holds that the goal of general education is to train the intellect, and the primary means to be the study of great books,

---

*The asterisk denotes that the reference may be found in Basic Readings, Chapter 2.

"books which have through the centuries attained the dimensions of classics" and are "contemporary in every age." The teaching is to be done by faculty members with wide-ranging intellectual interests who are devoted to this form of undergraduate instruction.

Hutchins was enough of a sociologist to realize that the modern university was not hospitable to his version of general education, and he leveled many criticisms in what turned out to be a losing battle with academic progress. He argued that the university had become too utilitarian by offering subjects which were vocational in nature and by employing faculty whose interests were in research rather than teaching or whose talents centered in narrow, specialized topics rather than broadly gauged issues. He maintained that universities had adopted a mechanical system of quantifying instruction and counting credit units that served to undermine education and accused them of accepting an extracurriulum that diverted attention from the substance of education. For these reasons, he found it necessary to create a separate college at the University of Chicago that functioned somewhat like an enclave for general education, while the rest of the university went about its business.

Kerr has been called the philosopher of the modern university* (Levine, 1978, p. 279), in large part because of his recognition of academic pluralism. The multiversity, he writes

> ...is not one community but several—the community of the undergraduate and the community of the graduate; the community of the humanist, the community of the social scientist, and the community of the scientist; the communities of the professional schools; the community of all the non-academic personnel; the community of the administrators... A community, like the medieval communities of masters and students, should have common interests; in the multiversity, they are quite varied, even conflicting. A community should have a soul, a single animating principle; the multiversity has several. (pp. 18-19)

Such an organization can offer much in the way of learning opportunities, for both students and faculty but, like life itself, it is also complex, confusing, and difficult to understand and control. Guided by a strong sense of pragmatism, Kerr has suggested modest improvements—not the radical restructuring demanded by Hutchins—that could be made in undergraduate education. He suggests a means to reward faculty for teaching at the undergraduate level, more attention to the preparation of generalists, and ways to individualize and personalize a large and complex university. As head of the Carnegie Council for Policy Studies in Higher Education, Kerr has done much to generate interest in renewing general education at the undergraduate level.

The idealism of Newman, progressivism of Whitehead, revisionism of Hutchins, and pragmatism of Kerr provide backdrop for contemporary debates about general education.

Ideas are seldom loftier than the actual programs by which they are given institutional form. General education in practice typically has meant some configuration of required courses, a number of free electives, and, in many cases, non-curricular activities and support services that further the goals of the curriculum.

Different concepts of general education have been given expression in various colleges and universities; three universities traditionally known for their general education programs are Columbia, Chicago, and Harvard. After World War I, Columbia established an interdisciplinary course on Peace Studies, later entitled Contemporary Civilization; required of all students, this four-semester course became the centerpiece of general education at the institution. Later, a year-long course simply called Humanities, consisting of a formidable reading list of primary sources, was added, as was a junior-senior colloquium, a two-year sequence available only to the very ablest students. A science course was also attempted but was abandoned. The fate of the program waxed and waned over the years, witnessing some of the most effective instruction and involving some of Columbia's "greats", such as Lionel Trilling, and at other times experiencing an exodus of senior faculty and decay in instruction. In 1966 Daniel Bell wrote the award-winning book *The Reforming of General Education* in an attempt to buttress general education, but his many cogent suggestions were not put into practice. A current analysis by Belknap and Kuhns (1977) discusses the history of general education at Columbia as well as some current efforts to enhance its effectiveness by means of a faculty seminar on general education and the creation of upper-division "teaching companies" organized around issues and problems that transcend departmental and disciplinary boundaries.

The University of Chicago was, of course, the laboratory for Hutchins to experiment with his ideas. Among the most important of its innovations were the development of a common core curriculum required of all students, a series of issue-oriented interdisciplinary courses, the creation of a separate faculty for teaching general education, and the admission of talented students before their graduation from high school. These concepts have been examined by Hutchins (1936), Bell (1966), and Levine* (1978).

Although the idea of a separate faculty has been abandoned, general education retains its original flavor at Chicago. About thirty percent of a student's studies consist of required core courses in the humanities, social sciences, physical sciences, and biological sciences. About the same number of additional general education courses are required of students, but the number and type vary depending on the their major field of specialization. The core courses rely on primary works, are organized and taught by interdisciplinary teams of faculty, and usually employ the seminar method of instruction.

Harvard has exercised influence more by what it has advocated than by what it actually has done. The report of a faculty committee, published in 1945 as *General Education in a Free Society* (and popularly known as the "Redbook"), became widely influential. It argued for core courses in which all students studied Western civilization, literary texts, scientific principles, and English composition. It also required students to take one additional course in each of the three divisions of humanities, social sciences, and natural sciences. Many of these courses were to be specially constructed interdisciplinary offerings. Although the Harvard faculty actually adopted only a modified version of this proposal, large numbers of colleges and universities around the country embraced the committee's proposals.

Although the best known programs tend to be at elite private universities, many other models have been utilized. During the last two decades a large number of state institutions were created, and several of these have developed distinctive approaches to general education. The University of Wisconsin-Green Bay has organized its program around ecological concerns; Evergreen State College in Olympia, Washington has fashioned a coordinated studies effort in which small groups of up to 100 students and five faculty study various thematic topics and grading is done by means of student portfolios; the University of California at Santa Cruz has adopted the cluster college structure to ameliorate the problems of impersonality and to provide students with alternative programs of general education. Some liberal arts colleges, such as Alverno and Mars Hill, have established competency-based programs, while others, such as Bethel in Kansas, have reinforced its Mennonite heritage by including studies of non-violence in its general education. Furthermore, community colleges such as Los Medanos in California, Rockland in New York, and Miami-Dade in Florida have developed their own forms of general education appropriate to their populist missions.

## CONTEMPORARY PERSPECTIVES

If general education is a timeless concern, it is also a timely one. It is an idea whose time has come again. Harvard once again has been propelled into a national leadership role in regard to general education with the appointment by Dean Henry Rosovsky of another faculty committee, the subsequent publication of its report, and the approval of the main features of its report by the faculty in 1978. However, unlike the reception of its predecessor in 1945, the "Harvard Plan" of today is being given mixed reviews elsewhere. Although most applaud the attention to general education, many writers in the academic as well as popular press are critical of the corrective measures proposed. Articles about these proposals in the *Harvard Gazette* (1978) and *Saturday Review* (1978), as well as criticism by Simmons (1979) and Botstein (1979), and comments by Sawhill (1979) and a group of educators in the *AAHE Bulletin* (1978), have signaled the emergence of a national debate about general education.

James Wilson, the Harvard professor who chaired the Task Force on the Core Curriculum, has declared (1978, p. 40), "...we do not see Harvard as a model for what all colleges ought to be." Yet he went on to note that:

> The emerging debate over curricular change has cast Harvard in the role of exemplar, assumed that whatever it did ought to represent the ideal, and criticized it for falling short of that ideal. The nature of that ideal differs, of course, depending on the identity of the critic: Kenneth Lynn, writing in *Commentary,* wishes we had created a more coherent, humanistic curriculum based on the great books; Henry Fairlie, in a syndicated column, berates us for not becoming more like an idealized Oxford; Alston Chase, writing in the *Atlantic,* worries that the liberal arts have been so subverted by relativistic social scientists and pandering to student wants as to make any curricular change suspect; and Barry O'Connell, writing in *Change...* protests

that elite colleges perpetuate social inequality, a tendency likely to be made worse by a core curriculum. Each has his own explanation as to why Harvard should have failed to attain the critic's personal ideal: departmental provincialism, philistine professors, weak administrators, the temper of the times, the rottenness of society, or whatever.

The points of contention revolving around the reform of general education are several. At the risk of oversimplification, many of the issues have been posed as polarities; several of the more salient of these are: Should there be few or many college requirements? Should there be a common core of courses that all students take, distribution requirements that allow students to select courses within specified areas, or free electives? Should the focus be on academic disciplines or on interdisciplinary topics, themes, or problems that more accurately mirror the real world? Should a general education course emphasize the content or the modes of inquiry of a field? Should the program be centered on subject matter or students? Should the subject matter be theoretical and abstract from everyday life, or should it be practical and connected with daily experience? Should courses convey only knowledge or should they explore the value implications of that knowledge? Is general education simply a matter of the curriculum and the classroom, or does it also include factors that transcend these formal contexts?

The current debate is often intense, sometimes bitter. In part, this is because people are operating in different educational contexts which have very different educational problems which require different solutions. Also disagreements exist because some seek to return to the "golden days" before the student protests led to the relaxation or abandonment of curricular requirements during the 1960's. Others seek to assert the value of the liberal arts after the job market led students to embrace careerism during the 1970's. Some seek a renewed emphasis on fundamentals by stressing basic skills in a time of declining student abilities in the three R's. Others are concerned with the need to reassert ethics and values in a post-Watergate era. And a number of people would like more emphasis placed on the common heritage and problems of humanity in an individual-oriented era characterized by the Proposition 13 movement. Still others would like the curriculum to be more concerned with the acquisition of a higher order of intellectual skills, the insertion of more substance into courses, and higher standards of accomplishment. Many, of course, prefer the maintenance of the status quo. In short, there is a great deal of ferment and little agreement. After a period of neglect, directions for the reconstruction of general education for our time are needed now. All of the earlier concepts are useful, but none are sufficient.

Fortunately, not all of the problems mentioned above exist at every institution. Furthermore, some consensus exists or is being created on many campuses about ways to improve the quality of general education in their particular contexts. The responses that large numbers of individual institutions make to these competing pressures may well contribute to the development of a new philosophy of general education for our time and provide contemporary approaches to this timeless topic.

Directions for the reconstruction of general education may be obtained from a careful analysis of changes in postsecondary education which have occurred since the last time concerted national attention was focused on this matter—the years immediately after World War II. Educators at that time found inspiration in Harvard's *General Education in a Free Society* for the creation of a host of programs. Since then many changes have taken place in higher education, not to mention in society, and several new approaches to general education are emerging that are markedly different from those of the past.

Demographic changes have implications for the revision of general education. Private colleges and universities, numerically and influentially dominant in 1945, have been eclipsed by the development of a much more differentiated system of higher education. Vastly increased numbers of students are now served by an array of community colleges, state colleges and universities, professional and technical schools, proprietary schools, and external degree programs. Today private institutions enroll less than one quarter of all students in colleges and universities. Programs devised at leading private institutions may no longer be useful models for other institutions, as they once were when the system was more homogeneous. There is no longer, if there ever was, a single model of effective general education.

In particular, public community colleges scarcely existed during the post-World War II days, but today they enroll approximately 36 percent of all undergraduate students. When one considers that general education traditionally has been the province of the first two years of college, an even larger portion of all general education today is being provided by community colleges. These institutions, unlike the elite private colleges are, for the most part, more attuned to community needs and have larger numbers of first-generation college students who are more vocationally oriented, more likely to attend on a part-time basis, and more oriented toward practical learning rather than abstract thinking. If general education is to have a rebirth, new approaches will have to be devised that are appropriate for these schools, their missions, and their students. Cohen (1978) has made a case for general education in the community college, and many such schools are developing promising programs.

Another important demographic change has been the increase in numbers of college students as well as a vast increase in their diversity. Today larger numbers of women, ethnic minorities, adults, part-time, poorly prepared, foreign, and handicapped students are enrolled; while not all of these students are found in equal numbers in all institutions, it is now rare that an institution is not affected by this broadened base of students. Thus, it is no longer possible for a teacher to assume that students are adequately prepared, strongly motivated, or able to benefit from the subject matter or instructional methods traditionally associated with general education. Rather, there is a need to devise ways to realize the traditional values of general education (e.g., abandonment of parochial views, acquisition of critical thinking abilities, and development of sophisticated tastes) for these non-traditional students. Although the goals may remain the same, the methods of achieving them will no doubt have to be different. (See Chapter 4 on "Objectives for Students" for further discussion.)

A tremendous expansion of professional education has taken place in recent years in colleges and universities and has forced new definitions of relationships between liberal arts and the professions. This ascendency of career education within the academy has paralleled the trend toward professionalization of work throughout society. One logical result of these shifts is that liberal arts courses are increasingly tailored to the particular interests and concerns of various vocational groups. Such courses as medical ethics, history of science and technology, and law and public policy are making an appearance in professional study. The University of Florida program called Humanistic Perspectives on the Professions has developed several special undergraduate courses related to the health, legal, engineering, and business professions. Although it seems not to have happened yet, one may expect the reverse to occur. That is, general education programs, which traditionally have contained only liberal arts courses, may someday incorporate components drawn from the professions. The classical professions of medicine, education, and religion, for example, if taught as part of general education rather than as career preparation, could deal profitably with the body and its health, including such topics as nutrition, exercise, and drugs; educational principles involved in such pursuits as parenting, schooling, and adult development; and spiritual and emotional well-being, such as those now treated by popular self-improvement books. These are vital topics that are of concern to Americans of all ages and circumstances.

Several cultural changes also have implications for contemporary approaches to general education. For example, following World War II, the United States was concerned primarily with Europe. Citizens wanted to understand why Germany, perhaps the most advanced nation at that time in Western Europe, initiated such a holocaust, how a repetition could be prevented, and what was needed to rebuild devastated nations. It was no accident that integrated Western civilization courses became central features of general education then. Today, however, a larger global perspective is needed with special emphasis on non-Western cultures, because our nation is facing significant problems in Asia, Africa, the Middle East, and South America—geographical and cultural areas in which many Americans are relatively unschooled. Although some institutions are resurrecting Western civilization requirements, others, such as St. Joseph's College in Indiana and the Massachusetts Community College Consortium, are incorporating more global perspectives by means of courses or modules dealing with non-Western cultures.

Further, it used to be accepted, at least implicitly, that a college education could provide a student with most of the basic knowledge, perspectives and principles he would need to live a fruitful life. The student was a vessel which college instruction filled with knowledge. This "container approach" appears to be giving way to one that emphasizes lifelong learning. Many have recognized that adults make changes, perhaps several times, in their families, vocations, and other parts of their lives which require new learning. In the adoption of a lifelong learning approach, it becomes critical that students learn how to learn, that is, to acquire learning techniques, problem solving abilities, and cognitive skills. Unlike their earlier counterparts, general education programs today often include courses that teach skills rather than solely subject matter. The Foundations for Learning program at the University of Rhode Island and the Introduction to Liberal Studies sequence at the College of St. Teresa are examples of this new thrust, as they stress lifelong learning skills such as critical thinking, communication ability, and quantitative thinking.

A lack of consensus about the aims and procedures of education has become evident in recent decades (Riley, 1978). No longer is it possible to proclaim that there is a body of knowledge that every learned person must master; the intellectual world is simply too vast and too differentiated for such a statement to carry authority today. As a result, some institutions are establishing programs in which students are expected to learn the methods of inquiry in different fields, that is, the ways various types of scholars think about issues, rather than simply the content of those fields. The "modes of thought" program at Brown University is one example of this approach to general education.

Other factors, too, are leading to approaches to general education that were not discussed by the authors of the "Redbook". Traditionally, general education has been regarded as a base or foundation on which to build a major field of specialization. Today a conceptual shift is occurring. some are using different metaphors, for instance, as a context within which the specialization is understood. Upper division courses are now being devised in which students learn how their specializations fit into a larger spectrum of knowledge, examine the utility of theories in practical settings, explore value implications of their knowledge, integrate knowledge around real world issues or problems, or note the limitations of their specialties. The interdisciplinary baccalaureate essay at Hobart and William Smith Colleges, the senior capstone seminars at several schools and the "teaching companies" at Columbia are illustrative of this trend toward upper division integrative offerings. The development of these upper division courses has been given impetus at some schools by the realization of many four-year institutions that they must provide general education for their increasing numbers of transfer students.

It is a truism that the complexity of academic life has increased, largely because of the increase in size, purposes, and number of programs at most institutions. Several institutions have seen their faculties embroiled in intense debate about the *single* best program of general education they can offer without recognizing that any single program is a procrustean bed. Given the variety of interests and purposes that exist among the students as well as faculty at any moderately large institution, it is possible to cope with complexity by thinking pluralistically. No single program of general education is likely to be as effective as several alternative programs, each of which is targeted as precisely as possible to a particular group of individuals. The Federated Learning Communities at the State University of New York at Stony Brook; subcolleges such as the Paracollege at St. Olaf College; and even more ambitiously, the cluster college structure at Grand Valley State Colleges represent promising pluralistic endeavors.

Further, since the 1950's, there has been an enormous amount of research conducted on the impact of college on students, some of which has contradicted the assumptions on which general education traditionally has been based. While most debates among faculty members consist of whether one or another course should be required, the research on student growth and development indicates that the curriculum and teaching of courses may have relatively little impact on the value outcomes of general education.

(See Chapter 6 on "Non-Curricular Dimensions" for further details.) The peer group, the residence hall, and informal contact between students and teachers as well as among students often are key sources of influence in broadening a student's ideas or perspectives and liberating him from parochial viewpoints. Today, the revision of general education is able to draw upon this extensive body of knowledge. If contemporary reformers are responsive to this scholarship, they will think beyond curricular changes alone and devise those opportunities for human interaction both in and beyond the classroom which have been shown to have the potential for promoting general or liberal education outcomes in students. Examples of efforts to stretch general education beyond the curriculum are: intentional living-learning environments such as the Residential College, University of Michigan; out-of-class learning opportunities such as at the New Center for Learning at East Texas State University; and experiential learning as in the internship program at LaGuardia Community College.

Some reforms have implications for the strategies of academic change, something that was absent from the Harvard report of 1945. The primary way in which new programs were developed and implemented during earlier years was by addition: new faculty were hired, budgets were increased, students were recruited, and new programs were appended to existing ones. Given the enrollment projections, funding prospects and hiring possibilities, this route to reform is simply not available to most institutions today. Rather, change must be wrought from within the limits of existing resources and faculty. New programs today are being introduced by shifting priorities, reallocating resources, reassigning faculty members, and developing the professional competence of existing personnel. (See Chapter 8 on "Initiating and Implementing Change" for elaboration.) This is a much more complicated procedure than reform by addition, and it requires that faculty development, broadly conceived, become part and parcel of curricular development. Numerous colleges and universities have established programs to help faculty recognize the need for renewing general education and for examining larger numbers of alternatives than they otherwise would consider, as well as to help them implement distinctive programs in which faculty are expected to play new and unfamiliar roles. Pacific Lutheran University, for example, engaged in a great deal of faculty development as its Integrated Studies Program, an alternate core curriculum, was being established.

The careful and sustained attention to the reconstruction of general education has just begun, and the thinking is very much in the formative stage. Each institution will have to determine what kind of general education is best, given its students, faculty, mission, history, character, and resources. But the reconsideration of educational ideals, historical perspectives, and contemporary realities is already leading to new approaches to general education that are appropriate for our times.

## ANNOTATED BIBLIOGRAPHY

American Association for Higher Education "Congratulations, But . . . ." *AAHE Bulletin*, September, 1978, pp. 3-7.
    Intended to spark debate about general education and to transcend the conceptual limits of

the Harvard report, several leading thinkers comment briefly on that plan. Reactors include Thomas Maher, John Stevenson, Theodore Newcomb, Joseph Katz, Mildred Henry, Warren Martin, Verne Stadtman, and Jonathan Warren.

Bailey, S. "Needed Changes in Liberal Education." *Educational Record*, 58 Summer, 1977, pp. 250-58.
Bailey sees the need to enhance liberal learning but is skeptical of efforts to reinstitute core courses and distribution requirements. Citing basic human needs of coping, working, and enhancing the free self, then drawing upon research on the life cycle, the author proposes ways to renew liberal education.

Belknap, R. and Kuhns, R. *Tradition and Innovation: General Education and the Reintegration of the University*. New York: Columbia University Press, 1977.
A report of a series of seminars on general education. Discusses changes in American higher education since World War II, problems engendered by these changes, ways Columbia has dealt with the curriculum during these years, and proposals for future curricular reform at the University.

Bell, D. *The Reforming of General Education*. New York: Columbia University Press, 1966.
A thorough analysis of the philosophy and sociology of general education, emphasizing the historically influential programs at Columbia, Harvard, and Chicago. Analyzes different conceptual styles of humanities, natural science, and social science, and proposes "third-tier" courses (beyond general surveys and major courses) to broaden a student's understanding of his/her major.

Botstein, L. "A Proper Education." *Harpers*, Sept. 1979, 33-37.
Author argues that liberal arts curricula now being revived are lacking in vision and that expressions of idealism often cleverly mask self-interest. He asserts that reforms should stress substance (rather than methods), especially the "central political and personal questions facing students;" liberal education could replace a portion of high school; and colleges should "disband a narrow departmental structure and stop emulating universities in their thinking, governance, and structure."

Cohen, A. "The Case for General Education in the Community Colleges." Unpublished paper available at the ERIC Clearinghouse for Junior Colleges, University of California, Los Angeles, Calif. 90024, 1978.
A carefully reasoned analysis of what general education is and might be within the context of community colleges. Contains sections dealing with what general education is *not*, criteria of useful programs, problems with general education, and suggestions of promising directions for revision.

Dewey, J. *Democracy and Education*. New York: Macmillan, 1963.
Written in 1915, this is a seminal work by a leading American intellectual and educator. Here Dewey applies his views of human nature, the social order, and philosophy to education and discusses the role of education in a democratic society. He argues that education must, above all, help individuals to organize and direct their experiences and to learn from them.

Dressel, P. *The Undergraduate Curriculum in Higher Education*. Washington, D.C.: Center for Applied Research in Education, 1963.
Although dated, this study presents perceptions of curricular planning that may be useful today. For instance, three different conceptions of breadth are identified: a) contact with the major divisions of knowledge; b) contact with different systems of value and with different cultures; and c) contact with the distinctive methodology of the various disciplines.

Harvard Committee. *General Education in a Free Society*. Cambridge, Mass.: Harvard University Press, 1945.
This influential book, sometimes referred to as "The Redbook," presents a theory of general education and contains discussions of its implications for secondary schools and the community, as well as for Harvard College. ". . .General education is distinguished from special education, not by subject matter, but in terms of method and outlook, no matter what the field."

Harvard Committee. *Report on the Core Curriculum*. Officer of the Dean, Faculty of Arts and Sciences, Harvard University, February, 1978.
Proposals for a core group of studies to be required of undergraduate students. Re-

quirements in several areas are proposed as well as a standing committee of the faculty to supervise the program by initiating, reviewing, modifying, and renewing courses offered in each area.

Hook, S., Kurtz, P., and Todorovich, M. *The Philosophy of the Curriculum: The Need for General Education*. Buffalo, N.Y.: Prometheus Books, 1975.
Contains major papers and critical commentaries developed in connection with a conference on this topic. Several perspectives are offered, including papers on general curricular issues and on specific issues within the humanities, natural sciences, and social sciences.

Hutchins, R. *The Higher Learning in America*. New Haven, Conn.: Yale University Press, 1936.
A series of four essays that contain many of Hutchin's ideas. General education, he maintains, is ". . .rightly understood as the cultivation of the intellect." He excludes ". . .body building and character building . . . the social graces and the tricks of the trade. . ." in favor of "permanent studies" as represented by the great books of the Western world.

Jaeger, W. *Paideia: The Ideals of Greek Culture*. New York: Oxford University Press, 1945.
A three-volume study that analyzes the historical process by which the Greek character was formed and the intellectual process by which the ideals of human personality and society were constructed. The role and nature of education are placed within this larger context.

Kerr, C. *The Uses of the University*. New York: Harper and Row, 1966.
A series of lectures which collectively argue that the modern university is actually a "multiversity" with many purposes, special interests, and social groupings. Asserts that the role of leadership is to mediate among these conflicting interests. Several proposals for improving undergraduate education within this context are offered.

Levine, A. and Weingart, J. *Reform of Undergraduate Education*. San Francisco: Jossey-Bass, 1973.
Discusses signficant innovations in curriculum structuring. Using institutional research data and interviews at 26 colleges and universities, authors analyze reform needs and efforts in undergraduate programs. Seven major areas of reform are targeted: academic advising, general education, comprehensive examinations, selection of majors, student-centered curriculum, alternatives to departments, and grading. Alternative curricular structures are discussed.

Marchland, B. "Reviving the Connected View." *Commonweal*, February 2, 1979, pp. 42-48.
Three proposals for reforming the liberal arts are offered. First, liberal education should impart the basic elements of cultural foundation; second, it should clarify and shape values; and third, it should teach learning skills.

McGrath, E. *General Education and the Plight of Modern Man*. Indianapolis: Lilly Endowment, 1976.
This is a statement by a long-term proponent of general education. Starting with an analysis of the human condition, he examines general education past and present and proposes improvements that need to be made. "In sum, to succeed today where it failed yesterday, the reshaping of general education must begin not with a consideration of subject matter but with human problems."

Newman, J. *The Idea of a University*. New York: Longmans, Green and Co., 1947 (Originally published, 1873).
This book by a leader of the Catholic Church in England has become a classic statement about liberal education. He asserts that the university ". . .is a place of teaching universal knowledge," implying that its essence is intellectual rather than moral and that it should be concerned with teaching rather than with scholarship.

Riley, G. "The Reform of General Education." Paper presented at conference of the Project on General Education Models, Marymount College, November, 1978. Available from author at the University of Richmond, Richmond, Virginia 23173.
Arguing that there is not a consensus about the aims of general education, the author articulates six quite different goals. He declares that ". . .without a systematic and critical review of the aims of education, colleges and universities will tend to reinstate mindlessly a 1950's model of general education. There is some evidence, in fact, that this is already happening."

Sawhill, J. "The Unlettered University." *Harper's,* February, 1979, pp. 35-40.
   Author decries the current state of liberal education and calls for reinstating its lost authority. "Limited, career-directed studies alone provide no lasting solutions to the multitude of
   difficult and potentially dangerous problems we confront. . . . Much of what must be accomplished may well require a radically different view of how we teach, what we teach, and
   whom we teach." Author declares that ". . .disregard for general education is an un-
   mitigated disaster."

Shulman, C. "Revamping Core Curricula." *AAHE Bulletin,* May, 1979, pp. 3-7
   A review of the current concern for core curricula, why there is so much interest, its role in
   undergraduate education, and a few sample programs.

Simmons, A. "Harvard Flunks a Test." *Harper's,* March, 1979, pp. 20-27.
   A hard-hitting criticism of the new "Harvard Plan" by the president of an innovative college. Argues that the reform proposals are timid and not sufficient as a model for the rest of
   higher education. Urges that each institution formulate its own general education program,
   that more innovative approaches be adopted, and that a diversity of programs is desirable.

*Toward the Restoration of the Liberal Arts Curriculum.* New York: Rockefeller Foundation,
1133 Avenue of the Americas, New York, N.Y., 10013, 1979.
   This is a series of background papers prepared for a conference and a summary of the
   discussion they elicited.

U.S. Office of Education *[Newman] Report on Higher Education.* Washington, D.C.: U.S.
Government Printing Office, 1971. Doc. No. HE5.250: 50065
   A comprehensive critique of higher education along with specific suggestions for improvement. This report of a small study group headed by Frank Newman helped define directions for improvement during the decade of the 1970's.

Veysey, L. "Stability and Experiment in the American Undergraduate Curriculum." In C.
Kaysen, ed. *Content and Context: Essays on College Education.* New York: McGraw-Hill,
1973.
   This lengthy essay provides a historic overview of the academic revolution after 1870;
   describes the reformers of the interwar period (e.g., Meiklejohn, Hutchins, and the
   Deweyans); the "shock waves" after World War II; and the formal components of the curriculum. Veysey gives priority to content over form.

Whitehead, A. *The Aims of Education.* New York: Macmillan, 1929.
   The content of education too often consists of "inert ideas," those that ". . .are merely
   received into the mind without being utilized, or tested, or thrown into fresh
   combinations." Argues that education should deal with the present and suggests that subjects and modes of study be taken when the person is at the proper stage of development,
   e.g., romance with the subject, precision, or the systematic study of a subject, and
   generalization, or the merger of romance with the precision gained.

# ADDITIONAL BIBLIOGRAPHY

Abel, E. "Liberal Learning: A Tradition With a Future." *Liberal Education,* May 1978,
   pp. 115-21.
Bailey, S. *The Purposes of Education.* Bloomington, Indiana: Phi Delta Kappa, 1976.
Bledstein, B.J. "Reassessing General Education." In D. Vermilye, ed., *Relating Work and
   Education.* San Francisco: Jossey-Bass, 1977.
Botstein, L. "Liberal Arts and the Core Curriculum: A Debate in the Dark." *Chronicle of
   Higher Education,* July 9, 1979, p. 18.
Brann, E. *Paradoxes of Education in a Republic.* Chicago: University of Chicago Press, 1979.
   1979, pp. 33-37.
Cahn, S. *Education and the Democratic Ideal.* Chicago: Nelson-Hall, 1979.
*Daedalus,* Volume I, Summer 1977; Volume II, Fall 1977. "Discoveries and Interpretations:
   Studies in Contemporary Scholarship."
Duncan, W. "Professional Education and the Liberating Tradition: An Action
   Alternative." *Liberal Education,* October, 1977, pp. 453-61.
Fincher, C. "Curricular Reform for the 1980's." *IHE Newsletter,* Institute of Higher
   Education, University of Georgia, September, 1978.

*Forum for Liberal Education.* "Ethics and Values in the Curriculum." Washington, D.C.: Association of American Colleges, March, 1978.

Garwood, J. "The Wrong Premise in General Education." *Intellect*, October, 1973, pp. 43-44.

*General Education in the Public University: Proceedings of a Conference.* Office of Academic Development, William Patterson College, Wayne, New Jersey 07470.

Good, R.C. "The Twenty-first Century Is Now." *Educational Record*, Winter, 1977, pp. 18-30.

Hall, J., ed. *Alternative Approaches to Curriculum.* Saratoga Springs, New York: Empire State College, in preparation.

Hammons, J. "General Education: A Missed Opportunity Returns." *New Directions for Community Colleges* 25, 1979, pp. 63-73.

Jencks, C. and Riesman, D. *The Academic Revolution.* New York: Doubleday, 1968.

Kaysen, C., et al. *Content and Context.* New York: McGraw-Hill, 1973.

Kornfield, M. "A New Opportunity for General Education." *Alternative Higher Education*, Summer, 1979, pp. 254-259.

Levine, A. "Ten Myths of General Education." *The Chronicle of Higher Education*, February 13, 1979, p. 56.

McGrath, E. *Values, Liberal Education, and National Destiny.* Indianapolis: Lilly Endowment, 1975.

National Center for Educational Statistics. *Digest of Educational Statistics 1977-78.* Washington, D.C.: U.S. Government Printing Office, Superintendent of Documents, Doc. No. 260-934/2039 1-3.

"New Approaches to General Education—II." *Forum for Liberal Education.* Washington, D.C.: Association of American Colleges, November, 1979.

O'Connell, B. "Where Does Harvard Lead Us?" *Change Magazine*, September, 1978, pp. 35-40.

Olson, P. *Concepts of Career and General Education.* AAHE/ERIC Higher Education Research report No. 8. Washington, D.C.: American Association for Higher Education, 1977.

"Programs for Intercultural Understanding." *Forum for Liberal Education.* Washington, D.C.: Association of American Colleges, January, 1979.

Regelski, T. "General Education in a Specialized World." *Phi Kappa Phi Journal*, Spring, 1978, pp. 34-37.

Reynolds, C. "Liberal and Technical-Professional Studies: A Societal Perspective on General Education." *Teaching-Learning Issues.* Learning Research Center: University of Tennessee, Knoxville, Tennessee, Fall, 1979.

Riesman, D., Gusfield, J., and Gamson, Z. *Academic Values and Mass Education.* New York: McGraw-Hill, 1975.

Rothblatt, S. *Traditional and Change in English Liberal Education: An Essay in History and Culture.* London: Faber, 1976.

Rudolph, F. *The American College and University: A History.* New York: Random House, 1965.

Sanford, N. *Where Colleges Fail.* San Francisco: Jossey-Bass, 1967.

Schiefelbein, S. "Confusion at Harvard; What Makes an 'Educated' Man?" *Saturday Review*, April 1, 1978, pp. 12-20.

Sullivan, E. and Suritz, P. *General Education and Associate Degrees: A National Study.* Washington, D.C.: American Council on Education, 1978.

Veysey, L. *The Emergence of the American University.* Chicago: University of Chicago Press, 1965.

Wegener, C. *Liberal Education and the Modern University.* Chicago: University of Chicago Press, 1978.

*What Ought to be Taught? The New Movement Toward General Education: Proceedings of a Conference.* Bard College, Annandale-on-the-Hudson, New York 12504, 1979.

Wilson, J. "Harvard's Core Curriculum: A View from the Inside." *Change Magazine*, November, 1978, pp. 40-43.

# 4.  Objectives for Students

## by Jerry G. Gaff

It is curious that most of the debate on general education is concerned with curricular philosophy, structures and subject matter, while little attention is given to students. The revision of general education is often carried out by faculty members and administrators without the meaningful involvement of students, and the discussions seldom reflect a sensitive and detailed understanding of students as persons and as learners. This chapter is devoted to the proposition that *who* is being taught should be at least as important as *what* is being taught among those who design and implement general education programs. A review of what is known about college students will precede the consideration of goals for their general education.

In the introduction to his landmark publication, *The American College*, Nevitt Sanford (1962, p. 1) observed:

> Practice in higher education, as in politics, remains largely untouched by the facts and principles of science. What our colleges do, tends either to be governed by tradition or to be improvised in the face of diverse—usually unanticipated—pressures. In the literature of the field there is much partisan argument, and little evidence on the basis of which conflicting claims might be evaluated. Very little is known of what particular features of the college environment determine such effects as have been observed.

This early volume summarizes what was known about college students at the time of its writing—what they were like, why they came to college, how they chose their schools, what learning experiences they had, how they changed during the college years, and what they were like as alumni.

In those days, the typical student was 18 to 21 years old, and had completed a college preparatory course of study in a secondary school. Also, this student was sufficiently talented to pass various admissions criteria, was academically oriented, and was more or less or motivated toward advanced study. Most students attended college full-time and lived in a campus residence. They were governed by *in loco parentis* rules formulated by the college largely without their participation, and were offered a curriculum that required them to take an array of liberal arts courses which were mostly taught by lectures or seminars.

Such a portrait seems quaint by today's standards. Not only have these college practices changed but they have been altered in large part because they are no longer suited to the kinds of students found in contemporary colleges and universities. The demise of this "boarding school" concept of higher education was brought on by several factors: legislation giving students the right to vote at age 18, reforms allowing students a legitimate role in the formulation of academic and social policies, provisions permitting part-time enrollment, protests against "irrelevant" courses and curricula, the relaxation of graduation requirements, and expansion of education beyond the campus.

## NON-TRADITIONAL STUDENTS

Perhaps the most significant change involved the nature of the students themselves. Driven by the ideal of equality of opportunity, and in recognition of the pivotal role a college education plays in one's future opportunities, policies at all levels of government were deliberarely fashioned to extend access to higher education to ever increasing numbers of individuals. Financial aid to needy students, special recruitment programs, open admissions, expansion of the number and types of postsecondary institutions, and the growth in size of existing institutions are illustrative policies which made access to institutions of higher learning easier.

It should come as no surprise that these various policies have greatly increased not only the number but also the diversity of students. Cross (1971) was one of the first to call attention to the new types of students. Defining the "new student" as one who scores in the bottom third of high school graduates on traditional tests of academic achievement, she declares that institutions of higher learning are not prepared to educate him. "Traditional education has failed him in the past; and unless substantial changes are made, it will fail him in the future." (p. xii) She presents evidence that

> New Students are positively attracted to careers and prefer to learn things that are tangible and useful. They tend not to value the academic model of higher education that is prized by faculty, preferring instead a vocational model that will teach them what they need to know to make a good living. New Students consistently pick the "non-academic" activities and competencies from among the lists that we present to them. New Students prefer watching television programs to reading; they prefer working with tools to working with numbers; they feel more competent in using a sewing machine than in reciting long passages from memory. New Students prefer to learn what others have said rather than to engage in intellectual questioning. New Students possess a more pragmatic, less questioning, more authoritarian system of values than traditional students. (p. 159)

This new student is not prepared to get a dose of Western civilization or to embark on a series of great books. Such familiar models of general education, however useful they may have been in the past and however appropriate they may be yet for some students, simply are not suited for these different kinds of students. Indeed, the prevalence of such students poses challenges to current curriculum designers, since they represent an entirely new factor. Just how general education can be designed and conducted so that it responds to this more pragmatic, less questioning student seeking a decent living is a question that needs to be taken seriously.

In her subsequent book about how colleges can best educate these low achievers, Cross *(1976, p. 27) cites "...five perceived causes of low academic achievement as the subject is revealed in the literature: 1) poor study habits; 2) inadequate mastery of basic academic skills; 3) low academic ability or low IQ; 4) psychological-motivational blocks to learning; and 5) socio-cultural factors relating to deprived family and school backgrounds." Programs to alleviate these difficulties have been established at many institutions, such as Harvard's Bureau of Study Counsel and the Learning Assistance Center at California State University at Long Beach.

Such programs include tutoring services, learning centers, and counseling programs (Maxwell, 1979; Roueche and Snow, 1977; Grant and Hoeber, 1978). Maxwell identifies several trends that are emerging to deal with poorly prepared students. These include the reinstatement of requirements for students to demonstrate their proficiency in reading, writing, and mathematics; increasing use of testing for better placement of students; development of more basic skills courses; and provisions of more academic support services, particularly learning assistance.

Most of the writers in this area argue that special programs on the periphery of an institution, by themselves, have little impact. What is needed to deal effectively with student needs is more responsiveness in the curriculum, the faculty, and the instructional methods. For instance, individualizing instruction by use of mastery learning, self-paced modules, and attention to various cognitive styles has been used with some success. (For more details on these instructional methods, see Chapter 7 on "Teaching and Advising".) There are, in other words, specific directions that hold promise for the education of certain students who, until recent times, have been excluded from higher education. However, these methods are not well known among faculty members who often lack the skills to apply these new instructional procedures. Hence, many experts call for faculty development programs to help instructors learn about the new students, how to teach them more effectively, and how to derive satisfaction from this kind of teaching. Indeed, Shaughnessy (1977) writes insightfully about what she is able to learn about the teaching of her subject from close attention to the ways her students understand the material.

Of course, other groups of "new" students are entering college who also pose serious challenges to traditional concepts of general education. Adults are perhaps the largest group. Once relegated to the periphery of an institution and enrolled in courses offered mostly in the evening, adult students have been propelled onto the center stage. Lifelong learning symbolizes an entirely new way of thinking about higher education, that is, that there are

*May be found in Basic Readings, Chapter 2.

times throughout life when anyone might need to achieve additional knowledge or skills, and colleges and universities are now important resources for adults (Knox, 1977). Peterson and his associates (1979) identify settings other than colleges or universities which offer learning opportunities; provide information about policies and programs in communities, states, and the federal government; and point to additional sources of information about lifelong learning.

In the Peterson volume, Cross (pp. 129-30), summarizing the characteristic needs and interests of adult learners, draws the following conclusions for programs planners:

> Adults are highly pragmatic learners. Vocationally and practically oriented education that leads to knowledge about how to *do* something is chosen by more adults than any other form of learning.... Traditional discipline-oriented subjects are not popular with the majority of potential learners.

> Better-educated and higher-income adults are much more likely to pursue so-called luxury learning in personal development or the use of leisure time, whereas disadvantaged learners are more interested in job training and in skill certificates.

> There seems to be a need for more active modes of learning. Whereas young people more or less expect to be told what to learn and expect to listen to "experts" dispense information, adults ordinarily want to be able to *use* the knowledge or skills learned.

Chickering and his colleagues (in press) have amassed a large amount of basic information about the education of adults. In the first part of his book, several scholars summarize what is known about development along intellectual, vocational, and moral dimensions, among others. A subsequent section deals with the significance of these theoretical analyses and research findings for the teaching of adults in various academic disciplines. A final section deals explicitly with implications for various academic practices—such as the curriculum, student services, and experiential learning—that will have to be modified in order to accomodate these new students.

Traditional practices of general education, most persons agree, are inappropriate for adults. Coherence is central to most general education programs, but what does curricular coherence mean for an adult who takes only one or two courses at a time? Also, older students have acquired a considerable amount of experience with the general culture and have developed their values in the context of making a host of adult decisions. What kind of education can be devised that builds upon this rich fund of life experience? There may be different foci of general education for late adolescents, persons in mid-life transition, and persons approaching retirement, or at least basic differences in the ways general education courses are conceived and taught.

Other types of students should be kept in mind when considering general education. A special issue of *Change Magazine* on the "Education of Black Americans" (October, 1979) is devoted to minority education and Black perspectives on such topics as desegregation, Black colleges, basic skills, and educational quality. Ballard (1973) has written persuasively about the special circumstances of Blacks and the ways colleges and universities must become more responsive to their needs. Ethnic studies, special curricula tailored to the interests of various minority groups, were introduced during the 1960's; although some programs have eroded, others remain vital. Today, special services such as financial, counseling, and learning assistance are often provided for minority students on predominantly White campuses. Gurin and Epps (1975, p. 403) have documented the contribution of the predominantly Black colleges to the education of students:

> Black students are motivated; they persist in college despite grave financial obstacles; they hold high career aspirations; they want graduate and professional education every bit as much as white students; they work more frequently and more hours and end college with greater indebtedness as proof of their educational commitments.

Women, too, have received attention as a distinct group. Astin and Hirsch (1978) assembled papers that deal with many aspects of women's education, including liberal arts education and women's development, the status of women's studies, characteristics of undergraduate women, and larger social issues. An earlier volume edited by Astin (1976) focuses on the continuing education of adult women, and women's studies programs have been examined by Blumhagen and Johnson (1978) and by Howe (1977).

Other groups, too numerous to discuss separately, have also received attention, including the handicapped, foreign students, and veterans. Each of these groups of traditional as well as non-traditional learners has its own distinctive needs and interests. They may require different kinds of curricula, modes of instruction, and support services to fully realize their human potential.

It should be abundantly clear from even this cursory review that the diversity of students cannot be well served by any single model of general education. This is especially true for certain traditional approaches to general education that were appropriate for earlier generations composed largely of white, male, middle class, eighteen-year-olds who were willing to go along with whatever professors taught. These realities can be ignored by curriculum planners only at their peril, for in the current buyer's market, students usually can find a school that will satisfy their desires, if not their needs.

## STAGES, STYLES, AND ENVIRONMENTS

The discussion of particular types of students tends to mask the fact that within each of these groups are differences with important educational implications. Three factors that cut across all student groups are their developmental stages, learning styles, and learning environments, each of which is discussed below.

Sanford articulates a theory of student development growing out of his earlier studies of the authoritarian personality. The lowest level of personality functioning is characterized by a kind of emotional-intellectual authoritarianism; this is a pattern in which strong impulses are held in check by a strong and rigid conscience moderated by a relatively weak and undifferentiated ego.

> This state of affairs at the core of the personality is reflected at the surface in characteristic ways: in stereotyped thinking, intolerance of ambiguity, punitive morality, submissiveness toward the powerful and dominance toward the weak, conventionality, anti-intellectualism, and hostility toward people perceived to be different from oneself. (1962, p. 261)

As students grow, as their egos gain strength and their consciences become less rigid, they usually learn to express their impulses in socially acceptable ways. They do less stereotypic thinking, acquire greater tolerance for ambiguity, and generally move away from authoritarian tendencies.

Other approaches to student development are being explored. Chickering* (1969) has devised a theory which posits that development can and should take place along seven vectors—achieving competence, managing emotions, becoming autonomous, establishing identity, freeing interpersonal relationships, clarifying purposes, and developing integrity. He has used this theory to understand the growing accumulation of empirical research and to suggest several ways colleges could more effectively promote growth among students. (See Chapter 6 on "Non-Curricular Dimensions".) As we have seen above, he is now extending this research to older students and studying development throughout the adult years.

Although most theorists and researchers on student development adopt some variation of neo-Freudianism, some couch their ideas in cognitive psychology. Following the pioneering work of Jean Piaget, who studied the development of reasoning in children, some scholars have examined the intellectual development of college students. Perhaps the best example of this approach is Perry's *Forms of Intellectual and Ethical Development in the College Years* (1970). At the lowest level of development the student thinks dualistically; there is truth and falsehood, good and bad, and there are authorities who present the truth to students (such as the teacher and the textbook). As students emerge from this stage, they think everything is relative, that there is no truth; naturally, then, there are no authorities, because each person's opinion is regarded as being as good as anyone else's. Finally, students may come to think that truth, while not absolute, is also not entirely capricious. There are truths within the context of assumptions, and informed persons using agreed upon methodologies can come to agreement about what is known and what is not. Most intellectual work is conducted at the highest level, but Perry stresses that the majority of students, particularly freshmen and sophomores, operate at one of the lower levels. The major point which is stressed by developmentalists is that the curriculum and instructional procedures should confront students at their own stage of development and attempt to advance them toward higher levels.

Several efforts, which are listed in the final section of this chapter, are underway to work with faculty and to devise specially tailored curricula that help students think in more sophisticated and complex ways. The Faculty and Student Development Project of Mildred Henry and Joseph Katz involves faculty members from several colleges in learning how to diagnose student learning modes and share ideas about how to move them to higher levels of thinking. The freshman seminars at the College of St. Teresa and Bloomfield College are means of concentrating on the classroom environment to promote more mature intellectual and personal development of students.

Another way to conceive of students is in terms of their learning styles. Claxton and Ralston (1978, p. 2) draw two conclusions from their summary of this topic:

> First, the findings underscore a fundamental fact of teaching and learning—students learn in different ways. The corollary is that teachers have particular learning styles as well. Second, student learning styles can be identified, and there are now tools available to help us do that.

Reichmann and Grasha (1974) identify six learning styles and develop a questionnaire to assess them. The styles are independent, dependent, collaborative, competitive, participant, and avoidant. Hill and Nunnery (1973) devise a scheme called cognitive mapping, in which a battery of tests identify such factors as preferred sensory modalities for learning (visual or auditory) and bases for making inferences (deductive reasoning, noting differences between objects and concepts, noting similarities among objects and concepts).

A more comprehensive scheme has been devised by Kolb (in press). Among other features, he identifies four learning styles. The "converger" works best on tasks for which there is a single clear answer to a question; his mind sorts through many facts to converge on the correct answer. The "diverger" is the opposite in that he is good at generating ideas, brainstorming, and imagining alternatives; he views situations and ideas from different perspectives. The "assimilator" likes to assemble diverse items into integrated wholes; this person is particularly adept at creating theoretical models and dealing with abstract concepts. The "accommodator" is impatient with abstractions and prefers to plunge into new situations and learn by trial and error; he is good at dealing with new circumstances and solving practical problems. Because each style has distinctive strengths and weaknesses, a student may encounter difficulties when confronted by a curriculum or a course that demands the learning styles he lacks. On the other hand, a general education could be designed to help students become competent in all four ways of learning.

Another way to think about students is in terms of their learning environments. The basic concept of the college as an environment for learning was set forth by Stern (1970) along with a questionnaire to assess students' perceptions of several elements within it. Pace (1969) developed another questionnaire, the *College and University Environment Scales*, that measures the amount of emphasis that students are able to perceive the school places on five factors—scholarship, awareness, community, propriety, and practicality. Other assessment techniques have been developed at the Educational Testing Service. For instance, the *Institutional Goals Inventory* assesses the consensus among students, faculty, administrators, and the community residents on purposes of the school, and the *Institutional Functioning Inventory* provides information about how the institution actually operates. All of these devices can be used not just to study the environment but to forge a consensus about changes that would enhance it. New general education programs might be more effective if planners carefully considered not just the courses but how their programs contribute to a larger environment that is conducive to learning.

## OBJECTIVES OF GENERAL EDUCATION

After the review of other aspects of students, it is possible to examine the objectives for students of general education. Just as there is a diversity among students, there is diversity among the aims and purposes of general education. Objectives, however, can be grouped into five major categories: 1) breadth of knowledge, usually achieved through some distribution requirement; 2) integration of knowledge across various disciplines or courses; 3) basic skills, such as the three R's; 4) advanced learning skills, such as literary, mathematical, statistical, and foreign language abilities; and 5) attitudes and values that are sometimes regarded as the marks of an educated person.

A 1947 report of the President's Commission on Higher Education that discusses the "objectives of general education" provides a useful benchmark; it says students are expected to:

1. Develop for the regulation of one's personal and civic life a code of behavior or ethical principles consistent with democratic ideals.

2. Participate actively as an informed and responsible citizen in solving the social, economic, and political problems of one's community, state, and nation.

3. Recognize the interdependence of the different peoples of the world and one's personal responsibility for fostering international understanding and peace.

4. Understand the common phenomena in one's physical environment, to apply habits of scientific thought to both personal and civic problems, and to appreciate the implications of scientific discoveries for human welfare.

5. Understand the ideas of others and to express one's own effectively.

6. Attain satisfactory emotional and social adjustment.

7. Maintain and improve one's own health and to cooperative actively and intelligently in solving community health problems.

8. Understand and enjoy literature, art, music, and other cultural activities as expressions of personal and social experience, and to participate to some extent in some form of creative activity.

9. Acquire the knowledge and attitudes basic to a satisfying family life.

10. Choose a socially useful and personally satisfying vocation that will permit one to use to the full his or her particular interests and abilities.

11. Acquire and use the skills and habits involved in critical and constructive thinking.

A more contemporary pamphlet (Branscomb, Milton, Richardson, and Spivey, 1977) provides another perspective. The authors declare:

> The general skills of writing, reading, speaking, and calculating are primarily the responsibility of elementary and secondary education. Mastery of these skills is essential for effective functioning in adult life as well as indispensible prerequisites for gaining a college education. Therefore these skills must be mastered by every student. (p. 5)

They continue:

> Besides such specific skills, basic understandings are necessary for intelligent adult behavior, no matter what one's vocation. In our judgment the concept of general education requires competence in a number of fields too frequently regarded as optional. While institutions may vary in level of expectation in these regards, we believe a general understanding of the concepts suggested under democracy and citizenship, history and geography, science, economics, literature, and self-directed learning is a must for all college graduates. (p. 10)

In addition, they argue that college graduates should be able to reason or think critically, have an informed acquaintance with the major methods of inquiry, acquire a penetrating knowledge of our form of government, exhibit a moral sensibility for both personal and institutional behaviors, and manifest a heightened sense of personal awareness.

Some individuals have given a good deal of thought to the ways such objectives should be formulated. A popular book (Mager, 1975) argues that objectives are most unambiguous and useful if they have four qualities: they should specify behaviors or capabilities in observable terms; state the behavior in terms of what a student can do (rather than what a faculty member teaches or covers); specify the circumstances under which the behavior is expected to be performed; and state the criterion level that will be used to evaluate performance. Although some criticize this approach as being mechanistic and simplistic, it does have the merit of specifying outcomes with sufficient clarity and precision so that they can be measured and educational accomplishment can be reasonably evaluated.

Two taxonomies of educational objectives, although well-worn, are still useful to individuals seeking to specify goals for students. Bloom and his associates (1956) devised a typology of cognitive learning that includes: knowledge (recall of facts or principles); comprehension (ability to restate ideas in student's own words); application (ability to use abstractions in specific circumstances); analysis (ability to separate material into its component parts); synthesis (ability to create wholes from parts); and evaluation (ability to judge properly the value of ideas). Krathwohl, et. al., (1964) turned their attenion to the more difficult affective domain and devised a similar set of categories.

One of the problems with articulating ambitious objectives for general education is that often they are not translated into the individual courses and teaching procedures adopted by the faculty. For example, Warren (1976) asked professors to describe what they wanted their students to learn in their courses. They most commonly listed analytical skills, the acquisition of knowledge, and problem-solving skills, but they gave little weight to synthesizing course content, generalizing learning to new contexts, engaging in intellectual inquiry, and fostering creativity—primary goals of general education.

At some colleges a deliberate attempt is made to translate agreed upon objectives into specific learning experiences. Those which feature competency based curricula, such as Alverno or Mars Hill Colleges, and those with individualized curricular contracts, such as Empire State College and University College at Memphis State University, are examples.

This chapter has attempted to stress that a sophisticated understanding of students is essential when it comes to considering general education, its goals and its improvement. Unless faculty and administrators are fully aware of students in their manifold diversity, the programs devised might turn out contrary to everyone's best interests. Indeed, given the projected decline in enrollments, serious consequences to whole institutions that do not consider student consumers can result. Sanford (1969, p. 197) has said it more positively and eloquently:

> ...Education aimed at developing the individual's potential as fully as possible is in the best sense *general education*. Introducing the students to a range of subjects and ideas, as in survey courses—sometimes called general education—is *not* the essential thing, though this may be a useful instrument of general education. Developing the generalist approach to inquiry, the synthetic function, is closer to the mark; and so is involvement in significant experiences with people and things. But this is by no means all. General education aims at development toward full humanity, and all the resources of a college should be organized to this end.

## PROGRAM EXAMPLES

Bloomfield College
Bloomfield, New Jersey 07003
Freshman Core Curriculum
William A. Sadler, Jr., Director

Two sets of interdisciplinary freshman courses have been designed to teach analysis and communication skills. One sequence focuses on the humanities and social sciences, and the other on mathematics and natural sciences. A Learning Support Workshop, that is actually part of the courses, provides assistance to students needing to improve their basic skills. There also are optional Life Planning Seminars aimed at developing self-confidence, self-awareness, and interpersonal skills.

Bronx Community College
City University of New York
Bronx, New York 10453
Networks
Richard A. Donovan, Project Director

How to develop and maintain an effective program for underprepared students has been the focus of a national project in which this school served as the resource institution. Knowledge, experience, and wisdom that has been gained at large numbers of institutions continues to be available to others who are concerned with effective education for these students. Conferences, technical assistance, and publications are major activities.

California State University
Long Beach, California 90840
Learning Assistance Center
Frank L. Christ, Coordinator

The LAC is a campus support system that mobilizes in one place information, personnel, equipment, and materials to serve learners who want "to learn more in less time with greater ease and confidence." It provides both drop-in and referral service in learning skills, offers individual and group assistance, and functions as a tutorial clearinghouse.

Colegio Cesar Chavez
Mount Angel, Oregon 97362
Irma Folores Gonzales, President

This institution is devoted to the advanced education of Mexican-Americans. A community-based, family-modeled, peer counseling system has been established to assist students in their college experience.

College of St. Teresa
Winona, Minnesota 55987
Freshman and Senior Seminars
Richard J. Weiland
Vice President for Academic Affairs

The year-long freshman seminar seeks to develop critical thinking skills by detailed attention to the nature of evidence, assumptions, and logic; to help students clarify their own values; to examine alternative philosophies of liberal learning; and to become oriented to college life. The senior seminar is likewise focused on students rather than predetermined subject matter as it explores the meaning of authenticity in human life in the face of an unknown future.

Empire State College
Saratoga Springs, New York 12866
James W. Hall, President

This entire college consists of a series of learning centers at which students and faculty members design individual curricula around the special needs and interests of students and the resources available in the college and community. Large numbers of adults are enrolled, many of them employed in regular jobs. A great deal of work has been done to hire and train faculty who are effective mentors in advising and teaching students, especially adults.

Illinois Central College
East Peoria, Illinois 61635
Development of Operational Reasoning Skills (DOORS)
Thomas C. Campbell, Project Director

This is a multidisciplinary freshman core course designed to improve students' reasoning abilities at this community college. It is based on Piaget's theory of intellectual development, and faculty members in different disciplines learn to prepare course material to enhance the cognitive skills of students. A careful evaluation of this and three similar cognitive-based programs is being undertaken.

Paideia
2701 8th Street
Berkeley, California 94720
Faculty and Student Development Project
Mildred M. Henry and Joseph Katz, Co-Directors

Undergraduate teachers from several colleges and universities are working cooperatively to diagnose student learning modes and devise learning tasks that advance students to higher stages of thinking. In seeking to apply available theory of student cognitive and affective development to regular classrooms, the project hopes to also promote the professional development of faculty members. Economical means for training faculty for improved teaching are expected.

St. Andrews Presbyterian College
Laurinburg, North Carolina 28352
Robert Claytor, Dean of Students

St. Andrews has developed not only a "least restrictive environment" for handicapped students but a full complement of peer aids and other supports to make the college as responsive to the personal and educational needs of handicapped students as possible.

University of California
Berkeley, California 94720
Bay Area Writing Project
James Gray, Director

This program is based on two assumptions: that there is no one best way to teach writing, and that much valuable information about how best to teach it is acquired by good teachers in their classrooms. This information is shared through institutes for faculty members, many of whom serve as "writing consultants" to their colleagues. Several other projects have been modeled on this effort at both higher and public school levels.

University of Chicago
Chicago, Illinois 60637
Quality and Accountability in Non-Traditional Education
Center for Continuing Education
Carol G. Schneider, Project Director

This is a consortium of colleges and universities with adult education programs that are seeking ways to enhance quality and accountability. A related emphasis is on developing alternative models for defining and monitoring student progress.

University of Nebraska
Lincoln, Nebraska 68588
Learning Analysis Course
Eugene P. Trani, Project Director

A three credit hour course, Learning Analysis, offers freshmen students units taught by faculty who excel at different methods, such as the Keller Plan, audio-tutorial, or discussion methods. Together, students and teachers explore alternative teaching-learning processes. A set of Student Learning Scales is being developed so that students can evaluate their own learning rather than the teaching of the faculty.

University of Rhode Island
Kingston, Rhode Island 02881
Foundations for Learning
College of Arts and Sciences
Gerry S. Tyler, Project Director

A series of five new courses that emphasize "generic skills" of liberal learning have been designed and taught as one portion of the renewed general education program. These include critical thinking in the humanities and in the social sciences, communication skills, experiencing the arts, and quantitative thinking skills.

University Without Walls
Loretto Heights College
Denver, Colorado 80236
Charlene Byers, Acting Program Director

Degree programs are individualized, with prior learning assessed and accredited, and studies organized to support both personal and vocational advancement. Also included here is an approach to liberal studies based on issues important to adulthood with seminars on the psychology of adult development, values in the adult experience, perspectives on the future, learning as adults, and career development.

## ANNOTATED BIBLIOGRAPHY

Astin, A. *Preventing Students from Dropping Out.* San Francisco: Jossey-Bass, 1975
Reports findings from a longitudinal and multi-institutional study of college dropouts. Contains information about student characteristics that predict dropping out, institutional factors that are related to withdrawal, and the impact of financial aid, employment, and residence policies on dropout rates.

Astin, H., ed. *Some Action of Her Own: The Adult Woman and Higher Education.* Lexington, Mass.: D.C. Heath, Lexington Books, 1976.
Describes the development and impact of 15 programs of continuing education for women. Authors include Elizabeth Cless, Carole Leland, Joseph Katz, and Jessie Bernard, who write about the programs and their effects on women, their families, and the institutions.

Astin, H. and Hirsch, W. *The Higher Education of Women*. New York: Praeger, 1978.
This is a series of essays in honor of Rosemary Park. In addition to the views of Park, the volume discusses women's colleges, women's development, and women's studies; university policies and practices toward women; academic women; and the women's movement in the national context.

Ballard, A. *The Education of Black Folk*. New York: Harper and Row, 1973.
A forceful call for equal educational opportunity for Blacks and a thoughtful critique of efforts to attend to their particular problems in colleges and universities.

Bisconti, A. and Solomon, L. *College Education on the Job: The Graduates' Viewpoint*. Bethlehem, Penn.: College Placement Council, 1979.
College graduates were asked to assess the usefulness of their college education to their careers. They found that "the majority of college graduates . . . do not think that college education prepares them to perform these activities (on their jobs)." Further, the respondents. . . "endorse, for their own jobs, courses that can enable one to communicate, figure, deal with one's fellow man, and understand economic affairs."

Bloom, B., ed., *Taxonomy of Educational Objectives: Vol. 1: Cognitive Domain*. New York: David McKay, 1956.
This is an old but still useful classification scheme of different ways of knowing. Six types of knowledge are identified: 1) knowledge (the recall of facts or principles); 2) comprehension (the ability to restate ideas in new words); 3) application (the ability to use abstractions in particular situations); 4) analysis (the ability to break material into its component parts); 5) synthesis (the ability to construct wholes from parts); and 6) evaluation (the ability to judge the worth of something).

Blumhagen, K. and Johnson, W. *Women's Studies*. Westport, Conn.: Greenwood Press, 1978.
This is a collection of articles analyzing various aspects of women's studies programs and issues of concern to women.

Branscomb, H., Milton, O., Richardson, J., and Spivey, H. *The Competent College Student*. Nashville, Tenn.: Tennessee Higher Education Commission, 1977.
This is a short, readable, and useful essay on the objectives and quality of higher education. Authors articulate forcefully and clearly what knowledge, skills, and personal attributes college graduates ought to possess.

Brown, K. "Sitting One's Way Through College." *Journal of Higher Education,* July-August, 1979, pp. 368-375. Reprinted from *Journal of Higher Education*, December, 1937, pp. 457-63.
A surprisingly contemporary plea for awarding a college degree on the basis of "worthy achievement." A thoughtful and cogent list of attributes of an educated person are presented which constitute a useful set of objectives for general education.

*Change Magazine:* Special Issue on the Education of Black Americans, October, 1979.
This entire issue is devoted to articles of relevance to minority education. Topics include desegregation, basic skills, Black studies and Black colleges, along with the usual array of reports, book reviews, and columns on research and Washington activities.

Chickering, A., ed. *The Future Ameican College*. San Francisco: Jossey-Bass, in press.
A comprehensive summary about what is known regarding education for adults. The first section contains articles by leading theorists and researchers on adult development; the second features implications for teaching adults in a variety of academic disciplines; and the final section stresses changes in college practices that will need to be made to accommodate the larger numbers of adult students.

Claxton, C. and Ralston, Y. *Learning Styles: Their Impact on Teaching and Administration*. AAHE/ERIC Higher Education Research Report No. 10. Washington, D.C.: American Association for Higher Education, 1978.
The authors review the concepts and research on several kinds of learning styles and argue that ways students learn should be given high priority in teaching and curricular matters. Suggestions about how this may be accomplished are given.

Cross, P. *Beyond the Open Door*. San Francisco: Jossey-Bass, 1971.
A study of the interests, abilities, and aspirations of "new" students who are not only taking advantage of open-door admissions policies but are enrolling in other institutions in

large numbers. Indicates ways these students are markedly different from traditional students and suggests educational programs that are responsive to their needs.

El-Khawas, E. "Putting the Student Consumer Issue in Perspective." *Educational Record* 58, Spring, 1977, pp. 169-79.

Highlights student rights, institutional responsibilities, and procedures to deal with consumer complaints and stresses the tendency for institutions to relate to students in a more businesslike and contractual manner. Changes are seen in judicial decisions affirming traditional consumer rights for students and federal requirements for institutions to make accurate disclosure of information on costs, descriptions of programs, faculty, and student dropout rates.

Grant, M. and Hoeber, D. *Basic Skills Programs: Are They Working?* AAHE/ERIC Higher Education Research Report No. 1. Washington, D.C.: American Association for Higher Education, 1978.

This booklet takes a look at basic skills programs that have been established in recent years. Suggestions for improvement are offered.

Gurin, P. and Epps, E. *Black Consciousness, Identity, and Achievement: A Study of Students in Historically Black Colleges.* New York: John Wiley, 1975.

Using data gathered in 1964, 1965, and 1970 and a longitudinal study of one freshman class, with data gathered in 1964, 1965, and 1968, three questions are addressed. The first centers on black students' attitudes toward their achievement as individuals: 80-90 percent want to enter a profession, but the level of aspiration for males is higher than for females. Second, the collective commitments and behavior of black students are addressed, especially in relation to civil rights and student rights movements. The third focus is on the problem of the student in reconciling individual and collective goals of achievement.

Haagen, C. *Venturing Beyond the Campus: Students Who Leave College.* Middletown, Conn.: Wesleyan University Press, 1977.

This is a study of students who interrupt their studies at a group of five small, primarily residential undergraduate colleges. Chapters analyze who leaves, for what reasons, what they do, the value of what they do, how many return, and what colleges can do to help this sizable number of individuals.

Heath, D. "What the Enduring Effects of Higher Education Tell Us About a Liberal Education." *Journal of Higher Education* 47, March/April, 1976, pp. 173-90.

An intensive interview study of 68 male graduates of an elite liberal arts college who are in their early thirties. In comparison with other factors in maturing, their college education did not have very important or pervasive effects on the lives of most. Suggestions for ways colleges might educate more powerfully are given.

Hill, J. and Nunnery, D. *The Educational Sciences.* Bloomfield Hills, Mich.: Oakland Community College Press, 1973.

An imaginative effort to develop a scientific language for education and to use it to describe the structure of thought. Tests provide results to "map" cognitive styles.

Hodgkinson, H. "Guess Who's Coming to College: New Learners, New Tasks." *NASPA Journal* 14, Summer, 1976, pp. 2-14.

Identifies changes in college practices that are occurring to accommodate increasing numbers of adult students. Elimination of residency requirements, extension of time campus is open, development of flexible adult degree programs, use of learning contracts, and provision of credit by examination or for experience are mentioned.

Howe, F. *Seven Years Later: Women's Studies Programs in 1976.* A report of the National Advisory Council on Women's Educational Programs, 1832 M Street, N.W., Washington, D.C. 20036, 1977.

This is a state of the art report prepared by one of the leaders in women's studies. Includes discussion of the curriculum, students, faculty and administrators, impact, and issues for the future.

Knefelkamp, L., Widick C., and Parker, C. "Applying New Developmental Findings." *New Directions for Student Services* 4. San Francisco: Jossey-Bass, 1978.

Summarizes major theorists concerned with cognitive and social-emotional growth during the college years and discusses how such knowledge can be applied, particularly by student service professionals.

Knox, A. *Adult Development and Learning: A Handbook on Individual Growth and Competence in the Adult Years for Education and the Helping Professions.* San Francisco: Jossey-Bass, 1977.

An encyclopedic synthesis and comprehensive survey of the current state of knowledge about adult learning and development. Concerned with understanding adults, whether faculty, administrators, or students. Chapters are organized around topics such as development during adulthood, context for development, and family role preference; education, work, and community performance; physical condition, personality, adult learning, women's roles, and adjusting to change.

Kolb, D. "Disciplinary Inquiry Norms and Student Learning Styles: Diverse Pathways for Growth." In A. Chickering, ed. *The Future American College.* San Francisco: Jossey-Bass, in press.

A rich conceptual model of learning styles. Discusses concrete experience and abstract conceptualization as two dimensions of the learning process, a model of experiential learning, and four different ways students tend to learn.

Krathwohl, D., Bloom, B., and Masia, B. *Taxonomy of Education Objectives: Vol. 2: Affective Domain.* New York: David McKay, 1964.

This volume contains a taxonomy for discussing affective or emotional objectives of education. Five categories are listed: 1) receiving (attention to feelings or values); 2) responding (some emotional or behavioral reaction); 3) valuing (acceptance or commitment to values); 4) organization (the construction of a value system); and 5) characterization (the development of a philosophy of life).

Mager, R. *Preparing Instructional Objectives.* 2d ed. Belmont, Calif.: Fearon, 1975.

A programmed text that spells out the need for establishing objectives and details the way they should be specified in order to be most useful.

Maxwell, M. *Improving Student Learning Skills.* San Francisco: Jossey-Bass, 1979.

This book is an extensive overview of practical steps to provide student services to students with learning difficulties. Written by a teacher "from the trenches," it discusses diagnoses of needs, various ways programs have been organized, and special problem areas (reading, writing, study skills, mathematics, science, and psychological barriers).

Morstain, B. "An Analysis of Students' Satisfaction with Their Academic Program." *Journal of Higher Education* 48, Janaury/February 1977, pp. 1-16.

Students who were least satisfied with their academic programs possessed a different educational orientation from students who expressed greater satisfaction. Dissatisfied students' attitudes also differed from faculty orientations. Dissatisfied students preferred more individually tailored or independent study learning situations, more collegial or egalitarian roles with faculty, and more informal and independent teaching and learning. The satisfied students preferred more formal or traditional teaching and learning models with more value attached to grades and external evaluations by faculty.

Perry, W. *Forms of Intellectual and Ethical Development in the College Years.* New York: Holt, Rinehart & Winston, 1970.

An in-depth study of students as they progressed through Harvard. Traces shifts in the ways they approached ideas and made ethical judgments and relates this to both developmental concepts and college experiences.

Peterson, R. and Associates, *Lifelong Learning in America.* San Francisco: Jossey-Bass, 1979.

This large volume takes a broad view of adult education. It examines the range of settings in which education is available; characteristics of adult learners; local, state, and federal policies and programs; information sources; and implications for the future.

Roueche, J. and Snow, J. *Overcoming Learning Problems: A Guide to Developmental Education in College.* San Francisco: Jossey-Bass, 1977.

Describes current remedial offerings after having studied nearly 300 two-or four-year institutions across the U.S. Determines that remedial education when coupled with effective teaching can save high-risk students from failure in college.

Sanford, N., ed. *The American College.* New York: John Wiley, 1962.

A massive classic work that deals with nearly all aspects of college life, particularly as they impinge on students. Chapters deal with such diverse topics as motivation in college attendance, characteristics of students in different types of schools and fields of study, the college environment, and dropouts.

Shaughnessy, M. *Errors and Expectations: A Guide for the Teacher of Basic Writing.* New York: Oxford University Press, 1977.

This book describes in detail the writing problems of students, elucidating the logic behind the errors that are made. The author found that close attention to these special problems taught her much about teaching and learning.

Solomon, L., Bisconti, A., and Ochsner, N. *College as a Training Ground for Jobs.* New York: Praeger, 1977.

Results of a longitudinal study of college-educated workers. Respondents rated their college education high in terms of general knowledge and credentialing their accomplishments. For developing career-related skills and competencies, leadership ability, and ability to think clearly, it received lower marks. College was regarded as even less helpful in directing students toward life goals.

Stern, G. *People in Context.* New York: John Wiley, 1970.

A basic text by a pioneer in conceptualizing and measuring various aspects of college environments and assessing their impacts on students.

Warren, J. "Describing College Graduates in 87 Phrases or Less." *Findings 3,* No. 2. Princeton, N.J.: Educational Testing Service, 1976, pp. 5-8.

Reports on studies of college graduates. One analysis deals with how faculty describe their best students. Another seeks to learn what faculty want students to learn from their courses. They most commonly list analytic skills, acquisition of knowledge, and problem-solving skills, leaving out synthesizing course content, generalizing beyond the immediate context, intellectual inquiry, and originality.

## ADDITIONAL BIBLIOGRAPHY

"ADAPT: A Piagetian-based Program for College Freshmen." *Research in Education,* University of Nebraska-Lincoln, Neb. 68588. 1976, ERIC ED 147 845.

Bloom, B., ed. *Taxonomy of Educational Objectives: Vol. 1: Cognitive Domain.* New York: David McKay, 1956.

Carnegie Commission on Higher Education. *Opportunities for Women in Higher Education.* New York: McGraw-Hill, 1973.

Clarenbach, K. *Educational Needs of Rural Women and Girls.* A report of the National Advisory Council on Women's Educational Programs, 1832 M Street, N.W., Washington, D.C., 20036, 1977.

*College Education and Employment—The Recent Graduates.* College Placement Council Foundation, P.O. Box 2263, Bethlehem, Pa. 18001.

*Designing for Development: Four Programs for Adult Undergraduates.* Denver, Colo.: University Without Walls Project Transition, Loretto Heights College, n.d.

Entwistle, E. and Hounsell, D. eds. *How Students Learn.* Institute for Research and Development in Post Compulsory Education, University of Lancaster, England, 1975.

Feldman, R. " 'The Educated Person'—Just What Does That Mean?" *Populi,* 6, No. 1, 1979, 19-27.

*Forum for Liberal Education.* "Liberal Education for Adults." Washington, D.C.: Association of American Colleges, October, 1978.

Hull, W. *Foreign Students in the United States of America.* New York: Praeger, 1978.

Knowles, M. *Self-Directed Learning: A Guide for Learners and Teachers.* New York: Association Press, 1975.

Krathwohl, D., Bloom, B., and Masia, B. *Taxonomy of Educational Objectives: Vol. 2: Affective Domain.* New York: David McKay, 1964.

Lauter, P. and Howe, F. *The Women's Movement: Impact on the Campus and Curriculum.* National Conference Paper Series. Washington, D.C.: American Association for Higher Education, 1978.

Lehrfield, J. "Two Programs of Liberal Education: A Commonplace Analysis." *Journal of General Education,* Winter, 1979, pp. 255-66.

Magill, S. "The Aims of Liberal Education in the Post-Modern World." *Liberal Education,* February, 1978, 435-442.

Newcomb, T., et al. *Persistence and Change: Bennington College and Its Students after Twenty-Five Years.* New York: John Wiley, 1967.

Pace, C. *College University Environment Scales.* 2d. ed., Princeton, New Jersey: Educational Testing Service, 1969.

Pernal, M. "Has Student Consumerism Gone Too Far?" *College Board Review* 104, Summer, 1977, pp. 2-5.

Peterson, R. "The Institutional Goals Inventory in Contemporary Context." *New Directions for Institutional Research* 19, 1978, pp. 31-47.

President's Commission on Higher Education. *Higher Education for American Democracy.* New York: Harper and Row, 1947.

Reichman, S. and Grasha, A. "A Rational Approach to Developing and Assessing the Construct Validity of a Student Learning Styles Instrument." *Journal of Psychology* 87, 1974, pp. 213-23.

Sanford, N. *Where Colleges Fail.* San Francisco: Jossey-Bass, 1969.

Spaeth, J. and Greeley, A. *Recent Alumni and Higher Education: A Survey of College Graduates.* New York: McGraw-Hill, 1970.

Taylor, H. *The World as Teacher.* Garden City, New York: Doubleday, 1969.

Tinto, V. "Dropouts from Higher Education: A Theoretical Synthesis of Recent Research." *Review of Educational Research*, Winter, 1975, pp. 89-126.

Tough, A. "Major Learning Efforts: Recent Research and Future Directions." *Adult Education,* Summer, 1978, 250-263.

# 5. Curricular Approaches to General Education

## Jerry M. Chance

General education is a complex matter, involving instruction, advisement, organization, administration, extra-curricular aspects, orientation, and placement. The spotlight, however, most often is directed toward the curriculum. This is because the curriculum constitutes the program of studies purposely designed as the major intellectual instrument for the achievement of the ends of general education. As will become apparent, rigorous thinking even about this single aspect is more complex than many would-be reformers realize. This chapter will discuss, first, several elements of the general education curriculum—philosophical assumptions, content, courses, matters of quantity and sequence, and structure—and stress that they are interrelated parts of a system. Second, it will consider issues in curricular design and offer several guidelines for curricular planners. Finally, a few types of general education programs will be described.

Three basic propositions underlie this discussion: 1) There is no single model of general education; several alternative approaches, in fact, are apparently effective; 2) A uniform program of general studies for all institutions of higher education is out of the question; each institution must devise its own curriculum to be congruent with its own circumstances; and 3) Simplistic curricular proposals to cure many real and fancied educational ills abound, and they are to be avoided.

## CURRICULUM: A SYSTEM AND ITS COMPONENTS

Axelrod (1968) in a little known paper discussed by Pfnister (1976, pp. 176-77) observed that the lack of long-lasting results of many innovations is due to the failure of the designers to view in broad perspective all that is involved in changing the curriculum. Changes often founder precisely because the systematic character of the curriculum is neglected. There is, Axelrod maintains, "...a certain reciprocity between each element in the system and all the other elements..., and before we can successfully reform one aspect of the process, we must understand profoundly the connections between it and the other elements in the system." For example, he identifies

49

six elements: content, schedule, certification, group/person interaction, student experience, and freedom/control. The first three of these elements he calls "structural" because they are under the direct and conscious control of the faculty; the latter three are regarded as "implemental" because they are conditions under which the first three factors operate. Although some may posit different elements, the important point is that several elements need to be considered together in order to have the best chance of success. A recent book by Conrad (1978) elaborates the systemic character of the curriculum and presents a framework for planning on this basis.

*Philosophy.* Among the most important curricular elements are the underlying philosophic assumptions and rationale, since the assumptions one makes at the outset of any inquiry play a large part in determining the results. Implicit in most programs of general education is the assumption that certain forms of ignorance are unacceptable for graduating college students (Belknap and Kuhns, 1977). Stated positively, general education often reflects the conviction of faculty and administrators that students ought to possess certain "minimally indispensable" kinds of knowledge (Hook, 1975). This assumption leads to the specification of key fields of study which contain that knowledge, or to the development of a special core curriculum in which certain basic courses are required of all students* (Boyer and Kaplan, 1977).

However, recent thinking reflects three alternative assumptions which compete with the so-called common body of knowledge. First, some thinkers stress method-of-knowing over what-is-known; hence "modes of thought" courses have appeared which seek to examine the thought processes and methods of inquiry found in different academic disciplines. The second alternative focuses on the achievement of certain goals or objectives rather than on the cognitive content and stresses that there are many ways by which such objectives may be attained in addition to taking regularly scheduled courses. The favored curricular approaches flowing from this assumption are those grouped under the competency-based label (Grant, et al., 1979). A third assumption shifts the common core of undergraduate education away from a common body of knowledge toward "common experiences, common problems, common exposures to reality and the larger society" (Rice, 1972). With this assumption, general education is not so much a body of knowledge or even a set of clearly specified student competencies as a set of common learning experiences, not exclusively in the classroom. The living-learning arrangements at the Residential College, University of Michigan, and the work experiences for students at Antioch College are examples.

Another philosophic issue is the assumed conflict between breadth, usually defined as general education, and depth, usually defined as a major. Both are vital aspects of a full education, but sometimes individuals speaking for general education are assumed to be opposed to specialization. Over a decade ago, Kolb (1966) tried to lay this issue to rest when he declared:

> We are *not* placing breadth and depth in opposition to one another....Modern man is a specialist and specialization re-

---

*May be found in Basic Readings, Chapter 2.

quires knowledge of a particular discipline or profession. But such depth itself becomes a form of dilettantism unless, standing in his specialty, the specialist sees his work as related to his life, his discipline as related to other disciplines, and his knowledge as related to the world of action and value. If this is breadth, it is also a more profound depth—a depth without which we cannot hope to live in the modern world.

But in order to allay the concerns of specialists, most reformers go out of their way to assure their colleagues that they regard general education to be compatible with specialization.

*Content.* The content is perhaps the most important element of the curriculum as Veysey (1973) declares. He maintains that "a historical examination...can show the deceptiveness of much of the apparent change and movement" that have been touted as reforms in higher education. The varying sizes and shapes of the curricular boxes, which have been highlighted in some reforms, are relatively minor when compared to the content of those boxes.

What is that content which infuses general education? One answer can be gleaned from a few titles of books on general education: *General Education in a Free Society* (Harvard Committee, 1945), *Educating for Survival* (Boyer and Kaplan, 1977), *General Education and the Plight of Modern Man* (McGrath, 1976), *General Education in a Changing Society* (Lukenbill and McCabe, 1978). Such works highlight profound social and individual concerns and place general education at their disposal. The content of these works stresses important contributions to understanding the human condition and to promoting the quality of life within the society and, indeed, around the globe. Although the specific content may vary from time to time and place to place, these issues affecting all of our lives—not simply surveys of selected academic disciplines—constitute the substance of general education.

Another response to the content issue can be obtained from philosophers who have studied the topic. For examples, Phenix (1964) argues that man is a meaning-seeking creature and that he has come to experience significant, but incomplete, meaning in six different realms. These realms of meaning have provided the occasion for the construction of corresponding bodies of knowledge. Further, each of the several bodies of knowledge is accumulated and validated according to its own epistemology, its own evidential system. The six spheres of meaning have the following corresponding bodies of knowledge: *symbolics,* primarily language and mathematics; *empirics,* physical, social and life sciences, and psychology; *aesthetics,* music, visual arts, arts of movement, and literature; *synnoetics*, psychology, literature and religion, expressed existentially; *ethics,* the varied special areas of moral and ethical concern; and *synoptics*, history, religion, and philosophy. Phenix claims that any meaning which enters the human experience will fall within one or more of the six generic categories. Consequently, he contends that the six realms of meaning, their bodies of knowledge and their methodologies, constitute "the basic competencies that general education should develop in every person." Hirst (1974) criticizes Phenix's paradigm, in large part because he believes disciplines encompass more than one realm of meaning, that they are not so internally consistent as Phenix assumes.

Three content areas of general education have been identified by the Carnegie Foundation for the Advancement of Teaching *(1977, pp. 165-179): 1) *advanced study skills* necessary for pursuing fields of knowledge at sophisticated levels; 2) *distributive studies* which enable the student to have breadth of understanding of the major subject and disciplinary fields; and 3) *integrative studies* which aim for a holistic, interdisciplinary understanding of various problems or issues. The authors are particularly distressed about the lack of attention to the first and third components. They note the decline during recent years in students' skills in writing, mathematics, and foreign language, and urge that cognitive skills be stressed in current reforms. The incoherence of distribution and elective courses is deplored, and integrative learning in which students "take broad approaches to understanding" is strongly recommended. Obviously, different steps are needed to strengthen each of these different areas of general education.

The reports of curriculum committees often reflect compromises about the content of general education. Harvard University, for example, recently has decided to require students to select eight from 80-100 specially designated courses in five major areas: literature and the arts, history, social and philosophical analysis, science and mathematics, and foreign cultures. Of course, such a list, which resembles those emerging from other general education committees, deals mostly with the distribution component of general education. The advanced learning skills and especially integrative learning, two key components of general education identified by the Carnegie Foundation, are neglected in many efforts to decide which content is to be required.

Other perspectives on the content of general education can be obtained from special focus groups. For example, there has been a great deal of interest in experiential learning in recent years, and many institutions have incorporated aspects of this non-classroom learning in their general education programs (Lupton, 1979). Whether through foreign travel (Eskow, 1978), community studies (Hursh and Borzak, 1979), internships, or other devices, experiences beyond the campus for academic credit have been shown to be powerfully transforming for students. Advocates of experiential as well as other innovative approaches can enrich the quality of thinking about the content of general education.

*Courses.* Whatever philosophy and subject matter are agreed upon, individual courses in many respects are the building blocks of a general education curriculum. A curriculum, however creative or distinctive, is only as strong as the courses that compose it. In one sense, virtually any course can be taught in a generally useful way for non-majors or in a technical and sophisticated way for students concentrating in that area. As Berry (1977) puts it, liberal (or general) education is an attitude and an approach to a course; it is not defined as consisting simply of certain specified fields of study, such as the humanities.

Large numbers of new courses have been fashioned to teach cognitive skills, offer distribution courses for non-majors, and provide integrative learning opportunities. Many examples of innovative courses in each of these components are given in two directories, *Selected Project Descriptions: Division of Education Programs* compiled by the National Endowment for the Humanities (1977), and *Ethics and Values in Science and Technology: A Resource Directory* compiled by the American Association for the Advancement of Science (1978).

Some schools have sought to define criteria that can be used to determine whether a given course is suitable for general education purposes. A curriculum committee at Bucknell University (1979), for instance, proposes that all general education courses satisfy four criteria:

1. The courses must attend to fundamental issues. That is, they must make explicit the presuppositions, procedures, basic modes of analysis, achievements, limitations, and/or central styles that are pertinent to an arena.

2. They must be comparative in character. Comparison is needed to introduce students to relativity of perspective, limitation of method, and distinctiveness of approach. Courses in general education should bring students to an appreciation of contrast and controversy over presuppositions and procedures.

3. The courses must concern themselves with the history or development of the area of knowledge in the course, and, in doing so, they will appropriately employ classic or important texts, works, or methods. Such works are largely primary sources that are rich in suggestiveness, that effect a turning point in thought and expression, and that enable one to discern most basically what is going on in a particular arena of exploration.

4. They must contain some form of constructive expression. In most cases, the appropriate form of constructive expression will be writing. But in any case, general education courses should enable students to bring their insights, ideas, and learning to clear statement by instructing them in the skills needed for that purpose.

*Quantity, Sequence, Timing.* Matters of quantity, sequence, and timing also are considerations in general education curriculum. At the beginning of American undergraduate education, general education consisted of virtually the entire curriculum, but gradually, especially following the onset of specialization in the latter half of the nineteenth century, the proportion of general studies in the entire four-year curriculum started to shrink. A noticeable reduction has appeared quite recently. In 1967 the proportion averaged about 43 percent, according to a national study (Blackburn, et al., 1976); during the next seven years, the proportion of general education continued to decline in the face of both relaxed requirements and "required electives" until it then represented, on the average, approximately one-third of the total undergraduate curriculum. This is roughly the same proportion as devoted to major requirements and to electives. Of course, these proportions vary considerably among institutions and even among fields within a single institution.

General education, particularly the study skills and distributive components, has traditionally been relegated to the first two years of college. The rationale for this arrangement is that symbolistic skills belong at the very beginning of the undergraduate career so that students have the abilities to pursue advanced learning. Also, distributive studies usually come very early inasmuch as the breadth of exposure to many disciplines facilitates a more informed choice in regard to the selection of a concentration. Finally, integrative studies taken toward the end of the undergraduate program help to place the concentration in a larger historical, cultural, and interdisciplinary context, thus alleviating undue narrowness and fragmentation of learning.

Despite the conventional wisdom of this pattern, new configurations are emerging. For one thing, general education sometimes extends throughout all four years of the college career. If integrative learning is valuable, it should not be left entirely to the last two years; further, that practice would completely rule out integrative learning experiences at certain institutions, for example, two-year community colleges. For this reason, freshman seminars and lower-division interdisciplinary courses are offered at several institutions. Although it may be reasonable for some basic skill courses, such as those emphasizing reading and writing, to be structured early in a career, other skills, such as statistics, may be better offered when students see them as a means of pursuing more specialized studies. Many different patterns for arranging the timing and sequence of general studies are, therefore, starting to appear.

*Structure.* Another curricular element is structure, both formal and informal. The formal structure consists of such identifiable parts as courses, modes of presenting courses (lectures, tutorials, off-campus experiences), grades, units of time (length of classes and length of terms), systems of numbering and awarding course credit, modes of sponsorship of courses (department, division, school), and larger schemes of courses (concentrations and clusters). Structural factors are important because they impose constraints on certain kinds of learning and provide opportunities for other kinds. For instance, if the formal structure consists entirely of 50-minute courses which are all taught within classrooms, opportunities for experiential learning are minimized.

Although the formal structure claims the bulk of the attention of curriculum committees, several scholars have stressed the importance of the informal structure. So powerful are the norms, expectations, and values of the college, the students, and the faculty that Snyder (1971) labeled them the "hidden curriculum." The educational potential of campus peer groups, dormitory life, student activities, student-faculty interaction, campus cultural events, advising, and counseling is too often ignored by general education reformers. This may be a serious mistake, because the research literature on the changes in students during the college years strongly points to the importance of these factors. Feldman and Newcomb (1969, p. 330), summarizing the results, declare, "...college faculties do not appear to be responsible for campus-wide impact (on students) except in settings where the influence of student peers and of faculty complement and reinforce one another." This topic will be elaborated more fully in the following chapter.

In summary, there are several elements of a curriculum, each of which is important in its own right—philosophical underpinnings, substantive content, courses, the quantity, sequence and timing of general education, and formal and informal structures. Yet, each element can impinge on the others in a number of ways. For example, if one seeks to address "real world" issues, such as world hunger, ethical issues in the life sciences, energy, or the quality of life, then multiple disciplinary perspectives will be valuable. An interdisciplinary program requires a sound philosophical rationale, a clear definition of the subject matter to be included, atention to how key themes will be incorporated within individual courses, determination about the proper amount and timing of such courses, and the creation of formal and informal structures to support the enterprise. Two common failings of interdisciplinary programs are that they lack a solid structure within the departmentally structured university, and that little attention is paid to the cultivation of a supportive informal network. The careful attention to the systemic quality of a curriculum can help avoid such failures.

## GUIDELINES FOR CURRICULAR DESIGN

Given the variety of elements and the systemic quality of a general education curriculum, how is a committee to go about redesigning this portion of a student's education? Several useful suggestions are offered by Wood and Davis (1978), including: 1) assessing the existing program by such means as analyzing student transcripts, testing for academic competency, and surveying current and former students and faculty; 2) exploring curricular options by studying programs at other colleges and universities; consulting with experts, and reviewing the published literature; 3) identifying curricular goals and obtaining agreement on them; 4) paying special attention to ways to implement the new plan; and 5) evaluating the new program to make midcourse corrections. Additional information and resources on initiation and implementation of changes may be found in Chapter 8.

Several general guidelines may be offered to curriculum planners. The first suggestion is that each institution tailor its general education program to its own character and traditions. The mission statements of each institution comprise one of the touchstones for this task. For instance, when Whittier College undertook a major curricular reform in 1970, it began with the writing of a philosophy of liberal arts education, but in doing so was careful to "retain the Quaker heritage which has always been an integral part of the Whittier experience" (Schambach, 1976). Contrariwise, one of the reasons cited for the difficulties of a radical curricular experiment at one university was allegedly due to failure of the curriculum "to take into account the character and traditions of the university" (Cass, 1974).

Sometimes these institutional factors run counter to the aims of general education. In such cases the general education curriculum may be so designed as to counterbalance or even to challenge limited institutional programs and assumptions. The interdisciplinary, intercollegial Cultural and Technological Studies program at the University of Wisconsin-Milwaukee was designed precisely to meet the general educational needs of engineering students who felt that the regular offerings in the humanities and social sciences did not adequately address the technological dimensions of the modern world. Initiated by the faculty of the College of Engineering and Applied Science, the CTS program brings together engineers, humanists, social scientists, and scientists to focus on the relationship between technology and culture as a common concern (Merritt and Drake, 1977).

Other basic reference points for designing a general education curriculum are widely recognized goal statements. A set of goals appropriate to the needs of society was provided by the Carnegie Foundation for the Advancement of Teaching *(1977, p. 159). These goals seem particularly relevant to the purposes of general education:

1. For its political well-being, society needs wise and effective leadership and an informed citizenry.

2. For its economic well-being, society needs able and imaginative men and women for the direction and operation of its institutions (broadly defined), for the production of goods and services, and for the management of its fiscal affairs. It also needs alert and informed consumers.

3. For its cultural advancement, society needs creative talent and appreciative and discriminating readers, viewers, and listeners. It also needs people who understand the common culture and its antecedents in other parts of the world.

4. For its survival, society needs members who understand the dependence of human beings on the resources provided in their natural environment and on one another.

5. For its moral and ethical integrity, society needs tone-setting models and persons who, as parents and teachers and in other capacities, are able to pass the nation's ideals and heritage along to future generations.

Other goals of general education for individual students may be found in the preceding chapter.

A third guideline concerns the conceptual framework of the curriculum. A clear and cogent theory of the curriculum elicits respect from the faculty, brings a sharper focus to the usually diffuse endeavors of the faculty and students in general education, contributes to a greater reinforcement and transferability of student learning, and promotes understanding by parents, legislators, and others in the larger community. Heavily biased and doctrinaire rationales, however, are not likely to command the broad support needed for success.

Because American higher education is pluralistic, one generally does not find any one of the many types of curricula existing in pure form. Hybridization, whether by design or not, more nearly represents the norm. The rationale of Concordia College's Core Curriculum reveals a thoughtful assessment of the competing curricular orientations and shows how a clear conceptual model can be achieved while avoiding the hazards of ideological purism (Your Friendly Neighborhood Core Committee, 1978-79).

A fourth guideline is that the general education program should be consistent with what is known about student development. The recognition of research findings regarding how college students learn and develop is a frequently neglected element in the design of general education curricula. One of the reasons for this is that professional researchers have not always revealed the practical implications of their findings for classroom instruction or for the management of the larger college environment; another is that curriculum planners often do not use what is known. Inasmuch as general education speaks the language of holistic development and aims at those kinds of learning which are of lifelong value, it seems imperative that curricular models reflect, at least implicitly, some of the generally accepted principles regarding human development and the conditions and processes of learning. Further, it is helpful for planners to have an understanding of the specific students enrolled at that school; a curriculum suitable for an Ivy League student body may be disastrous for students at a community college or at a technical institute. These issues are explored more fully in both the preceding and following chapters.

A final guideline calls for a careful consideration of specific obstacles and constraints concerning curricular change at the institution. A realistic appraisal of these hindrances is required, because a proposed curriculum model constructed in disregard of immovable objects is not likely to succeed. Whittier College's curricular planning committee, mentioned earlier, recognized at the outset certain inalterable restrictions on their work: 1) retention of the Quaker heritage; 2) a student body of approximately 1,800 students; 3) a faculty of no more than 110; and 4) no major changes in existing physical facilities (Schambach, 1976).

Every institution has its own peculiar set of conditions or forces not subject to alteration or elimination. Accepting such restrictions at the outset and making allowances for their impact on the curriculum will help prevent wasted time and possibly a fatal setback to the program. It should be pointed out, however, that colleges and universities are, in part, political institutions and therefore have the authority to imbue certain kinds of "immovable" objects with surprising tractability.

## TYPES OF PROGRAMS

Having reviewed a number of considerations in designing a general education program, it remains to examine a variety of curricular models. Eisner and Vallance (1974) discern and compare five competing orientations to the curriculum, which, allowing for modifications and intermingling, represent a conceptual spectrum within which most general education curricula may be found.

> 1. *The Cognitive Processes Approach* takes education to be primarily open-ended and growth-oriented. Disdaining curriculum content, proponents of this approach accentuate the *how* rather than the *what* of education. The chief concern is "that of sharpening the intellectual processes and developing a set of cognitive skills that can be applied to learning virtually anything."
>
> 2. *The Curriculum as Technology Approach,* like the cognitive processes approach, is concerned with the process of education rather than with its content. Yet its concern is *not* with the processes of knowing and learning but with the processes of technologically "facilitating" learning through systems design, input/output management, stimulus and reinforcement. It is an allegedly value-free application of industrial production techniques to the classroom.

3. *The Self-actualization, or Curriculum as Consummatory Experience Approach,* understands the curriculum as a context for stimulating personal integration and liberating, holistic development. It is growth-oriented and focused on the student. The curriculum should be a "liberating process," "enriching in its own right, and conducive to self-discovery and integrated experience."

4. *The Social Reconstruction-Relevance Approach* sees the curriculum in the context of its larger social setting. It has a reformist and futuristic approach to societal institutions, viewing the curriculum as a vehicle for producing change-oriented activists. On its more social-psychological side this approach seeks an enlightened accommodation between individual and society by fostering issue-awareness and survival skills in a rapidly changing world.

5. *The Academic Rationalism Approach* represents the more classical and traditional approach to the curriculum. The aim is to develop the student's intellect by providing access to the greatest ideas and achievements of man's intellectual and cultural heritage, particularly the Western tradition. It stresses adherence to the traditional disciplines of knowledge and development of the precision, generality, and potency of intellectual activity.

In "An Ecology of Academic Reform" Grant and Riesman (1975) define four curricular reform models, each based on different premises. These are referred to as telic reforms because each embodies a distinctive set of ends or purposes.

1. *The Neo-classical Model,* as exemplified in the Great Books approach at St. John's College, is "founded on the radical faith in the ability of liberal education to teach men and women to think for themselves and to become conscious of their social and moral obligations."

2. *The Aesthetic/Expressive Model,* personified by the legendary Black Mountain College and earlier versions of Bennington and Sarah Lawrence, stresses a non-verbal atmosphere in which academic disciplines supplement the arts, rather than vice versa.

3. *The Communal Expressive Model,* characterized by Kresge College, University of California, Santa Cruz, was designed to utilize a human relations approach to stimulate creativity and excitement through "open, direct, and explicit relationships."

4. *The Activist Radical Model,* illustrated by Antioch College, took at its end the critique of society and the preparation of students to be active participants in shaping their world.

These telic reforms are discussed in greater detail in Grant and Riesman's book, *The Perpetual Dream* (1978). Also included are discussions of several popular reforms. These are defined as "...changes in the character of undergraduate education brought about by increases in student autonomy, new patterns of organization, and attempts to respond to the demands of minority and other previously disenfranchised groups." Among the institutions analyzed in detail are New College and its eventual merger with the University of South Florida, the cluster colleges at the University of California at Santa Cruz, and two experimental state colleges in New Jersey—Ramapo and Stockton.

A different typology is proposed in Bergquist's chapter, "Eight Curricular Models" (in *Chickering, et al., 1977): heritage-based, thematic-based, competency-based, career-based, experience-based, student-based, values-based, and future-based models. A specific curriculum is described for each. Additional brief descriptions of various general education programs at different types of colleges and universities are contained in the October, 1977, November, 1978, and November 1979 issues of the *Forum for Liberal Education.*

As this review of programs indicates, there is no single model of general education. But there are many alternative approaches that abound, often with persuasive rationales and apparent success. These different types of programs might stimulate the imagination of members on a general education committee, while the sheer number of options can encourage them to follow their own best ideas wherever they lead. Viewing the curriculum as a system and attending to its several elements, utilizing a few principles of curricular design, and examining a number of different kinds of programs in operation at other schools should prove to be useful steps a committee can take in revising a general education curriculum.


## ANNOTATED BIBLIOGRAPHY

Bergquist, W. "Eight Curricular Models." In A. Chickering, et al. *Developing the College Curriculum.* Washington, D.C.: Council for the Advancement of Small Colleges, 1977, pp. 87-109.
    A discussion of various models, including those based on a study of heritage, themes, clearly defined competencies, career preparation, experiences, conceptions of student development, values, and future-responsiveness. Examples of each model are given.

Berry, D. "The Liberal Arts as Attitude." *Journal of General Education*, Fall, 1977, pp. 228-34.
    The author argues that "the liberal arts are not so much a body of knowledge or a selection of subject matters or disciplines, as a particular method and attitude . . . The question is not what bodies of knowledge we should provide. It should be true that all subjects (most?) can be studied in a liberal arts way."

Blackburn, R., Armstrong, E., Conrad, C. , Didham, J., and McKune, T. *Changing Practices in Undergraduate Instruction.* Berkeley, Calif.: Carnegie Council on Policy Studies in Higher Education, 2150 Shattuck Ave., Berkeley, Calif. 94704, 1976.
    This is a national survey of major changes in undergraduate education between 1967 and 1974 at two- and four-year colleges and universities.

Bowles, W. "Distribution Requirements and Student-Faculty Learning Needs." *Educational Record* 57, No. 4, 1976.
    This article zeroes in on the recent move toward a more structured undergraduate curriculum that includes distribution requirements is not based on the characteristics and needs of today's students and the world in which they will have to live. He outlines approaches to establishing distribution requirements that he believes would be useful and admonishes faculty to work out a new consensus on what is worthwhile to teach given the fact that the half-life of most 'knowledge' today is less than a decade.... If we persist on our present route, we will ensure that our students have built-in obsolescence."

Cohen, A. ed. "Shaping the Curriculum." *New Directions for Community Colleges* 25. San Francisco: Jossey-Bass, 1979.

This issue contains several articles on many aspects of the curriculum and its reform. Some items deal explicitly with general education and others with the process of change, program evaluation, statewide planning, and administrative strategies.

Concordia College. *Your Friendly Neighborhood Core Committee, 1978-79.* Mimeographed. Available from David M. Gring, Assistant Dean of the College, Concordia College, Moorhead, Minn. 56560.

A zesty but carefully reasoned description of Concordia's Core Curriculum, including sections on the rationale, administration, current courses, and application forms for the inclusion of new courses. The Concordia program has received national attention, and this document is well worth reviewing.

Conrad, C. *The Undergraduate Curriculum: A Guide to Innovation and Reform.* Boulder, Colo.: Westview, 1978.

This comprehensive handbook is designed to aid faculty, administrators, and students engaged in curriculum reform at the undergraduate level. Author proposes a systems model for curriculum planning and examines four major areas—general and liberal education, area concentration, experiential learning, and calendar and degree programs. For each area key issues are identified, strengths and weaknesses of different approaches are discussed, and a variety of innovations are cited.

*Curriculum Proposal, Third Draft.* Bucknell University, Lewisburg, Pa. 17837, January, 1979.

An in-house proposal for a new general education program that was submitted to the Curriculum Committee.

Dudley, J., ed. *Field Experience Education Casebook.* Manuscript available from the Council for the Advancement of Experiential Learning, Columbia, Md. 21044, in preparation.

Contains descriptions of the 11 field experience programs and a discussion of the contribution of field experience to college education. Issues related to developing and operating such programs are included.

Eisner, W. and Vallance, E., eds. *Conflicting Conceptions of Curriculum.* Berkeley, Calif.: McCutchan, 1974.

A collection of essays, written for the most part by college professors of education, which is organized around five dominant concepts which govern competing approaches to the curriculum. Although probably written for the training of school teachers, the material is sufficiently archetypal and conceptual as to be relevant to theorizing about college curricula.

Eskow, S. "Vagantes in the Community Colleges: Notes Toward a Populist Theory of Study Abroad." Paper delivered at a conference on International Education and the Community College, 1978. Available from Office of the President, Rockland Community College, Suffern, NY 10901.

This paper contains an argument in favor of the educational value of travel, the importance of community colleges' offering opportunities for international travel, and ways community colleges can provide such opportunities.

*Ethics and Values in Science and Technology: A Resource Directory.* Washington, D.C.: American Association for the Advancement of Science, 1978.

Very brief descriptions of over 900 courses and programs in science, technology and human values; environmental concerns; health care, life sciences, and behavioral sciences; industry, commerce, and society; and public policy making.

Grant, G. and Reisman, D. "An Ecology of Academic Reform." *Daedalus* 104, 11, Winter, 1975, pp. 166-91.

An interpretive analysis of four relatively recent "telic reforms" in higher education curricula. The authors cite these reforms as small but inordinately influential alternatives to the research-oriented multiversities.

Grant, G., et al. *On Competence.* San Francisco: Jossey-Bass, 1979.

This is a report of a four-year national study of competence-based education. It provides a rationale for competence-based programs and discusses how they affect teaching, curriculum, assessment, academic standards, and student learning. A team of scholars analyzes key issues and reports on the results at several institutions.

Hirst, P. *Knowledge and the Curriculum.* London: Routledge and Kegan Paul, 1974.
This is a philosophical analysis that deals with aspects of knowledge and their implications for the curriculum. Discusses conceptual and logical structures of knowledge, truth criteria, and methodology of various fields of study.

Hursh, B. and Borzak, L. "Toward Cognitive Development Through Field Studies." *Journal of Higher Education,* Jan./Feb., 1979, pp. 63-78.
A description of a field studies program and an evaluation of the impact on students who participated in it. Results document value of the program for the education of students involved. Concludes that ". . .the outcomes of this field study design appear to correspond well to forms of development valued in traditional, campus-based education."

Keeton, M. and Associates. *Experiential Learning: Rationale, Characteristics, and Assessment.* San Francisco: Jossey-Bass, 1976.
Analyzes current state of experiential learning and describes its characteristics. Discusses present and future means of measuring, assessing, and credentialing.

Koltai, L., ed. "Merging the Humanities." *New Directions for Community Colleges* 12. San Francisco: Jossey-Bass, 1975.
This sourcebook has articles written by faculty and administrators involved in various courses and programs that offer integrative education.

*Liberal Education,* Spring, 1979.
Issue focuses on the humanities and includes discussions of 10 recent innovative programs that have been funded by the National Endowment for the Humanities.

Lukenbill, J. and McCabe, R. *General Education in a Changing Society.* Dubuque, Iowa: Kendall/Hunt Publishing Co., 1978.
A report from Florida's Miami-Dade Community College about its extensive general education review conducted between 1975 and 1978. Emphasizes the process of formulating a working consensus on the character and goals for general education at this school, and describes the framework of the programs developed for various associate degrees. Includes a section on support services and an implementation plan complete with a timetable.

Lupton, D., ed. *Alternative Higher Education,* Spring 1979.
Special thematic issue devoted to experiential learning. Articles describe a variety of programs at several institutions.

Martin, W. "Alternative Approaches to Curricular Coherence." Paper presented at a conference on Coherence of the Curriculum, Empire State College, Saratoga Springs, N.Y., April, 1977. Available from the author at the Danforth Foundation, 222 South Central Ave., St. Louis, Mo. 63105.
Four conceptually distinct approaches to general education are presented. The "common fate" approach stresses common experiences or a shared heritage; the "common tools" approach seeks to provide students with skills and methods for their continual learning; the "common ground" approach seeks to find epistemological agreement among various academic disciplines; and the "uncommon individual" approach emphasizes the potential and unique qualities of individuals.

Mattfeld, J. "Toward a New Synthesis in Curricular Patterns of Undergraduate Education." *Liberal Education*, December, 1975, pp. 531-49.
The author provides a cursory overview of historical patterns of undergraduate curricula, gives examples of contemporary curricular alternatives, and argues that the needed synthesis in higher education curricula should be based on aesthetic and intuitive feeling as well as on rational processes.

Merritt, H. and Drake, D. "Technology and Cultural Values: Revitalizing an Undergraduate Humanities Curriculum." *The Journal of General Education* 29, Summer, 1977, pp. 141-51.
A descriptive account of the emergence of the NEH-funded Cultural and Technological Studies program at the University of Wisconsin-Milwaukee. Of particular interest is the conclusion of the engineering faculty and students that the regular humanities and social science general education courses were not relevant to their needs. The interdisciplinary CTS program functions as an alternative to standard humanities and social science requirements and has attracted large numbers of non-engineering students.

Mohrman, K., ed. "New Approaches to General Education." *Forum for Liberal Education*. Washington, D.C.: Association of American Colleges, November, 1978.

This newsletter describes programs at Brigham Young University, North Texas State University, St. Anselm's College, Bowdoin College, Gustavus Adolphus College, and Illinois Central College. Other resources are mentioned.

O'Connell, W., Jr. and Associates. *Improving Undergraduate Education in the South*. Atlanta: Southern Regional Educaton Board, 130 Sixth St., N.W., Atlanta, Ga. 30313, 1979.

A report of the results of a special project that used multiple methods to improve undergraduate education. Chapters discuss competency-based curricula, adult education, faculty development, staff development in the community college, instruction for undergraduates, faculty evaluation and institutional rewards, and strategies for institutional change.

Phenix, P. *Realms of Meaning*. New York: McGraw-Hill, 1968.

This is a "philosophical theory of the curriculum for general education based on the idea of logical patterns in disciplined understanding. The central thesis is that knowledge in the disciplines has patterns or structures and that an understanding of these typical forms is essential for teaching and learning. . . . The various patterns of knowledge are varieties of meaning, and the learning of these patterns is the clue to the effective realization of essential humanness through the curriculum of general education."

*Report on Teaching: 6*. New Rochelle, N.Y.: Change Magazine Press, 1977.

The last of six special reports on teaching highlights interdisciplinary programs and instruction. A variety of programs are discussed, several in some detail, including a skills course on the nature of evidence, a liberal arts program in a technical institute, an American studies program, a developmental approach to teaching science and mathematics, and an environmental thematic program. Other examples are briefly described.

Rice, G. "General Education: Has Its Time Come Again?" *Journal of Higher Education* 43, October, 1972, pp. 531-43.

Rice distinguishes between the "existential" and the "essentialistic" orientations to the curriculum. He finds that general education programs are shifting away from the latter (discipline-oriented) model to the former (experience-oriented) model, and he takes comfort in that shift. Of the temporal modalities, Rice stresses the priority of the present to either the past or the future. He furthers thinks curriculum designers should give emphasis to holistic theories of personality development.

Riesman, D. and Stadtman, V., eds. *Academic Transformation: Seventeen Institutions Under Pressure*. Sponsored by the Carnegie Commission on Higher Education. New York: McGraw-Hill, 1973.

Collection of essays describing events in a variety of colleges and universities during the turbulent 1960's. Most authors write from experience about the crises and their long-range effects in areas such as structural and curricular reform, student participation, and campus decision making. Institutions include Antioch, University of California at Berkeley, MIT, City College of the City University of New York, Federal City College, Swarthmore, and Old Westbury.

Schambach, R. "A Model for Curricular Change: The Whittier Experience". *Liberal Education*, October, 1976, pp. 401-6.

A brief but very helpful account of major curricular change which was undertaken at Whittier College. Illustrates the need for gaining consensus on a philosophical model prior to the development of a mechanical curricular model.

Schwab, J. *Science, Curriculum and Liberal Education*. Westbury, I. and Wilkof, N., eds. Chicago: University of Chicago Press, 1978.

This is a book of essays by a biologist who is deeply involved in general education at the University of Chicago. The essays reflect the author's insights into the role of science in liberal education.

Select Committee on the Curriculum. *Education at Amherst Reconsidered*. Amherst, Massachusetts: Amherst College Press, 1978.

This report seeks to build upon past accomplishments in its proposals for improvements. Several themes run through the report: "The special introductory function of a student's first year at college, the illiberality of either a narrowly specialized education or an education in which students establish no intellectual relationships among courses taken, the importance of a large measure of choice among studies, the dangers of exaggerated distinctions between disciplines or departments, the benefits of faculty members working together in planning and teaching courses, the rejection of passive absorption as a satisfactory mode of learning".

*Selected Project Descriptions: Division of Education Programs.* Washington, D.C.: National Endowment for the Humanities, 1977.
   Brief descriptions of 44 projects supported by NEH grants. The rationale, program description, and lessons learned are mentioned for each.

Tussman, J. *Experiment at Berkeley.* New York: Oxford, 1969
   A profound analysis of problems with traditional college curricula, and description of a significant alternative lower-division program based on the experimental college model developed at the University of Wisconsin by Alexander Meiklejohn. Although that school met its demise, its philosophy and struggles toward success contain important lessons for contemporary education.

Vander Meer, A. and Lyons, M. "Professional Fields and the Liberal Arts: 1958-78." *Educational Record*, Spring, 1979, pp. 197-201.
   A re-study of a well-known survey conducted by Dressel, Mayhew, and McGrath. Results showed professional faculty members in nine fields "are less favorably disposed toward the liberal arts today than were their counterparts in 1958." However, they "continue to be strongly in favor of the requirement of a liberal arts component in every curriculum."

Wood, L. and Davis, B. *Designing and Evaluating Higher Education Curricula.* AAHE-Eric/Higher Education Report No. 8. Washington, D.C.: American Association for Higher Education, 1978.
   An eclectic study of curriculum design and evaluation reflecting the experiences of the authors, both of whom work with faculty in these two areas. Among the topics discussed are the state of the art in design and evaluation, defining the curriculum, needs assessment, implementation, and the purposes of evaluation.

Zaltman, F., and Sikorski, A. *Dynamic Educational Change.* New York: The Free Press, 1977.
   This book transforms the results of academic research into a form useful to the practitioner. The first part of the book shows how schools are different from other types of complex organizations, and how certain of these distinctive aspects affect change in them. Key concepts in the book are planning change, linkage, and needs of clientele. In a closing chapter, 313 useful principles are derived from the previous 10 chapters.

## ADDITIONAL BIBLIOGRAPHY

Axelrod, J., "Curricular Change: A Model for Analysis." *Research Reporter.* Center for Research and Development in Higher Education, University of California, Berkeley, Ca. No. 3, 1968, 1-4.

Axelrod, J., In A. Pfinster. *Planning for Higher Education, Background and Application.* Boulder, Colorado: Westview Press, 1976, pp. 176-77.

Belknap, R. and Kuhns, R. *Tradition and Innovation : General Education and the Reintegration of the University.* New York: Columbia University, 1977.

Bergquist, W. "Responding to the Future Through Curricular Reform." *Liberal Education*, May, 1976, pp. 229-44.

Booth, W., ed. *The Knowledge Most Worth Having.* Chicago: University of Chicago Press, 1967.

Bordier, G., et al. *Curricular Revision: A Methodological Approach.* 1975. ERIC ED 121 229, EDRD.

Calabro, H. "Curricular Relevance for Today's Youth." *Improving College and University Teaching* (Hampshire College Program), 23, No. 1, Winter, 1975, pp. 49-50.

Cass, J. "Experiment with Radical Reform: New Curriculum at Brown University." *Saturday Review/World*, June 1, 1974, p. 49.

Cerny, R., et al. "Engineering Education: Classical Liberal Arts of the 70's." *Journal of the National Association of College Admissions Counselors*, 21, No. 4, June, 1977, pp. 1-6.

Chickering, A. *Experience and Learning.* New Rochelle, New York: Change Magazine Press, 1977.

Clark, B. *The Distinctive College: Antioch, Reed, and Swarthmore.* Chicago: Aldine, 1970.

Cohen, D. "Some Considerations in the Development, Implementation and Evaluation of Curricula." ERIC ED 098 075. September, 1974.

Collins, C. and Drexel, K. *General Education: The Los Medanos College Model*. Available from Los Medanos College, Pittsburg, California94565.

Counts, G. "Some Notes on the Foundations of Curriculum-Making." *Curriculum Theory Network*, 1975, pp. 281-94.

Curriculum Design and Development Course Team. *Curriculum Innovation*. Halstead Press, 1975.

DeMont, B. and DeMont, R. "The Commitment to Personalized Learning and Its Relationship to Student Behavior." *Liberal Education*, October, 1976, pp. 407-16.

*Designing a Core Curriculum*. Proceedings of an Institute on Core Curriculum Design, St. Joseph's College, Rensselaer, Indiana 47978, June, 1979.

Diorio, J. "Knowledge, Truth, and Power in the Curriculum." *Educational Theory,* 27, No. 2, Spring, 1977, pp. 103-10.

Dressel, P. *College and University Curriculum*. Berkeley, California: McCutchan, 1971.

Duley, J. and Gordon, S. *College Sponsored Experiential Learning: A CAEL Faculty Handbook*. Columbia, Maryland: Council for the Advancement of Experiential Learning, 1977.

Ewen, T. *Think Piece on CBE and Liberal Education*. CUE Project Occasional Paper Series No 1, May, 1977, Bowling Green State University, Bowling Green, Ohio.

Feldman, K. and Newcomb, T. *The Impact of College on Students*. San Francisco: Jossey-Bass, 1969.

Fethe, C. "Curriculum Theory: A Proposal for Unity." *Education Theory* 27, No. 2, Spring, 1977, pp. 96-102.

Fethe, C. "A Philosophical Model for Interdisciplinary Programs." *Liberal Education*, December, 1973, pp. 490-97.

*Forum for Liberal Education*. "Core Curriculum." Washington, D.C.: Association of American Colleges, October, 1978.

Friedman, E. "A New Composition Program for Oregon." *Freshman English News,* 5, No. 3, Winter, 1977, pp. 22-23.

Gaff, J. and Associates. *The Cluster College*. San Francisco: Jossey-Bass, 1970.

Gow, D. and Yeager, J. "The Design and Development of Individualized Curriculum Materials for Higher Education." *Journal of Higher Education*. January/February, 1975, pp. 41-54.

Harris, J. *Teaching-Learning Issues: Curriculum Innovation—Three Dimensions*. 1974. 15 pp. ERIC ED 112 777, EDRS.

Harvard Committee. *General Education in a Free Society*. Cambridge, Ma.: Harvard University Press, 1945.

Heil, J. "Teaching, Training, and the Liberal Arts Curriculum." *Liberal Education*. October, 1974, pp. 308-15.

Henderson, A. *The Innovative Spirit*. San Francisco: Jossey-Bass, 1970.

Hogges, R. *Curriculum and Instructional Processes in American Higher Education*. April, 1976. ERIC ED 127 858, EDRS.

Hook, S., Kurtz, P. and Todorovich. *The Philosophy of the Curriculum*. Buffalo, N.Y.: Prometheus Books, 1975.

"Interdisciplinary (That Much Abused Word)." *Teaching-Learning Issues*. Learning Research Center, University of Tennessee, Knoxville, Tennessee, Winter, 1976.

Jacobson, R. "Alverno's Experiment: The Dissidents and the Defenders." *The Chronicle of Higher Education*, June 26, 1978, pp. 3-4.

Katz, J. and Sanford, N. "Curriculum in the Perspective of the Theory of Personality Development." *The American College*, Nevitt Sanford, ed. New York: John Wiley, 1962.

Kaysen, C. "What Should Undergraduate Education Do?" *Daedalus*, February, 1974, pp. 180-85.

Knott, R. "What Is a Competence-Based Curriculum in the Liberal Arts?" *Journal of Higher Education*, January/February, 1975, pp. 25-40.

Koch, M. "Liberal Arts: Carrier Pigeon or Albatross?" *Community College Frontiers*, 6, No. 1, February, 1977, pp. 4-6.

Kockelmans, J., ed. *Interdisciplinarity and Higher Education*. University Park: Pennsylvania State University Press, 1978.

Kolb, W. "A College Plan Designed for Flexibility." In S. Sulkin, ed. *The Challenge of Curricular Change*. New York: College Entrance Examination Board, 1966.

Levensky, M. "Trying Hard: Interdisciplinary Programs at the Evergreen State College." *Alternative Higher Education* 2, Fall, 1977, pp. 41-46.

Levit, M., ed. *Curriculum: Readings in the Philosophy of Education*. Urbana, Illinois: University of Illinois Press, 1971.

Lottes, J. and McCray, E. *The Nature and Significance of Curricular Claims and How They are Validated*. ERIC ED 103 389, February, 1975.

MacDonald, G. *Five Experimental Colleges*. New York: Harper and Row, 1972.

Mayhew, L. and Ford, P. *Changing the Curriculum*. San Francisco: Jossey-Bass, 1971.

Mayville, W. *Interdisciplinarity: The Mutable Paradigm*. AAHE/ERIC Higher Education Research Report No. 9. Washington, D.C.: American Association for Higher Education, 1978.

McGrath, E. *General Education and the Plight of Modern Man*. Indianapolis: Lilly Endowment, 1976.

Middleburg, M. *Moral Education and Student Development During the College Years: A Selective Annotative Bibliography*. ERIC ED 146 882, EDRS.

Mohrman, K., ed. "The Core Curriculum." *Forum for Liberal Education*. Washington, D.C.: Association of American Colleges, October, 1977.

Morgan, G. "A New Interdisciplinary Curriculum." In Smith, G., ed., *New Teaching, New Learning*. San Francisco: Jossey-Bass, 1971.

Morstain, B. "An Analysis of Students' Satisfaction with their Academic Program." *Journal of Higher Education* 48, 1977, pp. 1-16.

Nash, P. "Gentrain: An Instructional Delivery System." *New Directions for Community Colleges*, Winter, 1975, pp. 49-56.

O'Connell, W., Jr., and Moomaw, W. *A CBC Primer: Competency-Based Curricula in General Undergraduate Programs*. Southern Regional Education Board, 1975.

Peterson, N. "Undergraduate Degree Programs: Assessing the Alternatives." Minneapolis: University of Minnesota, Center for Educational Development, 25 pp. Available from Center for Educational Development, 317 Walter Library, University of Minnesota, Minneapolis, Minn. 55455.

Petrie, H. "Do You See What I See? The Epistemology of Interdisciplinary Inquiry." *Journal of Aesthetic Education*, January, 1976, pp. 29-43.

Pfnister, A. *Planning for Higher Education*. Boulder, Colorado: Westview Press, 1976.

Phi Delta Kappa. *Education and the Structure of Knowledge*. Stanley Elam, ed. Chicago: Rand McNally, 1964.

Pinar, W., ed. *Curriculum Theorizing: The Reconceptualists*. Berkeley, California: McCutchan, 1975.

Posner, G. "The Extensiveness of Curriculum Structure: A Conceptual Scheme." *Review of Educational Research*, February, 1974, pp. 401-7.

Rice, E. *Idea Tasting*. Lexington, Ma.: Ginn Custom Publishing, 1979.

Romey, W. "Transdisciplinary, Problem-Centered Studies: Who is the Integrator?" *School Science and Mathematics*, January, 1975, pp. 30-38.

Shaffarzick, J. and Hampson, D. *Strategies for Curriculum Development*. Berkeley, California: McCutchan, 1975.

Schlesinger, M. *Restructuring General Education: An Examination of Assumptions, Practices, and Prospects*. CUE Project Occasional Paper Series No. 2. May, 1977, ERIC ED 142 102, EDRS.

Select Committee on Education, Academic Senate: University of California, Berkeley. *Education at Berkeley: The Muscatine Report*. Berkeley: The University of California Press, 1968.

Short, E. and Jennings, T., Jr. "Multidisciplinary: An Alternative Approach to Curriculum Thought." *Educational Leadership* 33, No. 8, May, 1976, pp. 590-94.

Sieben, J. *Competency-Based Education: Promise and Danger*. 1977. ERIC ED 147 821, EDRS.

Snyder, B. *The Hidden Curriculum*. New York: Knopf, 1971.

St. John's College *Bulletin 1978-79*. Annapolis, Maryland 21404.

Suddarth, B. "An Investigation of General Education Requirements in College Curricula." *Research in Higher Education* 3, No. 3, 1975, pp. 197-204.

Swick, K. "Components of an Effective Curricular Design for Teaching Culturally Different College Students." *College Student Journal*, November/December, 1974, pp. 6-9.

Toombs, W. "The Application of Design-Based Curriculum Analysis to General Education." *Higher Education Review*, 1978, pp. 18-29.

Trites, D., ed. "Planning the Future of the Undergraduate Curriculum." *New Directions for Higher Education* 9, Spring, 1975.

Veysey, L. "Stability and Experiment in the American Undergraduate Curriculum." In C. Kaysen, ed. *Content and Context: Essays on College Education.* New York: McGraw-Hill, 1973.

Vineyard, E. "General Education Component." *Community and Junior College Journal,* May, 1978, pp. 24-25.

Walker, D. "The Curriculum Field in Formation." *Curriculum Theory Network,* 1975, pp. 263-80.

Winston, M. "Reflections on Student Unrest, Institutional Response, and Curricular Change." *Dedalus,* February, 1974, pp. 212-216.

Wise, R. *The Use of Objectives in Curriculum Planning: A Critique of Planning by Objectives.* ERIC ED 103 956, April, 1975.

## PROGRAM EXAMPLES

There are so many different types of general education programs that all of them cannot be mentioned in this limited space. However, there are a number of institutional revisions that can serve as useful resources to others embarking on general education reform. The few schools listed here are included because their reforms reflect rich thinking about substantive issues in general education. Also, the revisions at these institutions are distant enough for them to have generated actual experience and perspective, and their programs are recent enough for their experiences to be transferred to their counterparts who are at earlier stages of the reform process.

Austin College
Sherman, Texas 75090
Harry E. Smith, President

A total institutional renewal effort has been undertaken, including a six-course interdisciplinary core curriculum as well as means for individualizing the educational experience for students throughout the curriculum. Other aspects of the overall renewal effort have included faculty development, a different academic calendar, and creation of an office of educational research and development.

Eckerd College
St. Petersburg, Florida 33733
Albert H. Carter, III, Associate Dean for General Education

A strong values emphasis pervades the distinctive general education offered at Eckerd, as a values sequence is taken by all students over all four years. Freshmen take two courses, "Inquiry and Human Nature" and "Values and the Search for Spirit"; the second year involves the examination of a world culture other than the student's own; in the last two years students choose from colloquia both in their major (to aid career preparation) and out of their major (to aid breadth of study).

Evergreen State College
Olympia, Washington 98505
Jeanne Hahn, Dean

The backbone of this program is coordinated studies, consisting of small clusters of up to 100 students and five faculty members. Each group focuses on different themes and issues that cross the usual disciplines. Individual learning opportunities and participative governance are other parts of the Evergreen program.

Grand Valley State Colleges
Allendale, Michigan 49401
Glenn Niemeyer, Vice President for Academic Affairs

Established during the 1960's, this state school opted to create a cluster of separate colleges, each with a separate curriculum and faculty. The group now includes four undergraduate colleges: College of Arts and Sciences; Seidman College of Business; William James College, with a stress on inter-disciplinary studies; and Kirkhof College with a focus on competency-based education.

LaGuardia Community College
City University of New York
Long Island City, New York 11101
Martin G. Moed, Dean of Faculty

All freshmen must fulfill an one-term internship in the community; sophomores must participate for two quarters. These work experiences are supplemented with campus seminars related to career planning, work-oriented value questions, and management skills. Another seminar involves students in independent research on work-related topics.

Los Medanos College
Pittsburg, California 94565
Charles C. Collins, Dean of Humanistic Studies

An open enrollment community college, Los Medanos has as its primary goal to help educate students to cope with those world problems which put their generation in jeopardy. Students are required to take six broad courses in each of six disciplinary areas, as well as two societal issues courses. The latter take an interdisciplinary perspective on such topics as ethnic concerns, ecology, and technology, including a self-directed study component within the structure.

Pacific Lutheran University
Tacoma, Washington 98447
Curtis E. Huber, Director, Integrated Studies Program

The Integrated Studies Program, an optional way for students to meet their general education requirements, offers a series of courses around the theme, "The Dynamics of Change." All courses are interdisciplinary, with new sequences being developed around faculty interests. Providing faculty development opportunities is an important component of this program.

Saint Joseph's College
Rensselaer, Indiana 47978
John P. Nichols, Coordinator, Core Curriculum

The Core Curriculum extends through all eight semesters of the college program, with components on study of the contemporary world, significant periods in Western culture, non-Western studies, man in the universe, and the application of Christian principles to the human situation. The college has an eight-semester writing program parallel to the Core; it hopes to do more to integrate residential life with the academic program.

St. Olaf College
The Paracollege
Northfield, Minnesota 55057
William R. Poehlmann, Senior Tutor

The Paracollege was created ten years ago as an experimental satellite of this small liberal arts college. With its own curricular offerings, faculty, administrator, and budget, this satellite was free to experiment with both the substance and form of general education and senior concentrations. It adopted a tutorial-examination system, a modification of the Oxbridge model. Now it operates as a regular option for St. Olaf students.

State University of New York
Stony Brook, New York 11790
Federated Learning Communities
Patrick J. Hill, Director

The eclipse of academic community is addressed with several novel integrative structures: the *federation* of thematically related courses into decentralized temporary educational units; a new kind of teaching professional, a *Master Learner,* who assists students in integrating the content and perspective of different disciplines in a new kind of course, a *Meta-Seminar*; and a team-taught *Core Course* in which the entire community of faculty and students attempts to forge a common language that defines issues. The themes to date have been "World Hunger," "Cities, Utopias, and Environment," "Technology, Values, and Society," and "Social and Ethical Issues in the Life Sciences."

University of Alabama
New College
University, Alabama 35486
Bernard Sloan, Dean

New College was created as a mechanism to personalize and individualize the education provided at this large university and to serve as a means to stimulating the professional development of faculty and renewal throughout the university. Individualized learning contracts, integrative seminars, and "growth contracts" for faculty are preferred means to these ends.

University of California
Berkeley, California 94720
Collegiate Seminar Program
Charles Muscatine, Director

Students are offered the chance to participate in intensive, small, interdisciplinary seminars. Subjects reflect the research interests of faculty as well as bearing significance to the lives and values of students. Instead of surveying a broad area, each seminar focuses on a new and relatively unexplored problem and allows students to learn the methods of different disciplines. Also, to the extent possible, the student conducts his or her own program of significant and innovative research.

University of California
Santa Cruz, California 95060
Eugene H. Cota-Robles, Vice President for Academic Affairs

Santa Cruz was designed as a distinctive campus within the University of California system, which incorporates the "cluster concept." Faculty have joint appointments to a discipline and a college, and the extra-curricular dimensions are given much attention at most of the colleges.

University of Wisconsin-Green Bay
Green Bay, Wisconsin 54302
Forrest Armstrong, Associate Professor of Urban Studies

Students are required to take nine credits in each of three areas: natural sciences, social sciences, and fine arts and humanities, with courses structured around the underlying epistemologies and distinctive methods and procedures of each area. At least six credits in each area must form an integrated sequence bringing students into sustained engagement with value questions inherent in social problems, especially as these questions are illuminated through cross-cultural comparisons. In addition, seniors enroll in interdisciplinary seminars addressing contemporary social and intellectual concerns.

Worcester Polytechnic Institute
Worcester, Massachusetts 01609
William Grogan, Dean

In an attempt to prepare students for the kinds of problems scientists and engineers face, WPI instituted a series of new requirements, two of which stress the relationship of social and personal values to technology. The Interactive Qualifying Project (equivalent to three or more courses) requires students to undertake a major project, such as defining and solving a local social problem, planning and involving social and technical issues, experiential field work, or historical analysis on a social problem. The humanities minor requirement immerses students in a single area, culminating in a final independent study essay.

# 6. Non-Curricular Dimensions of General Education

## By John P. Nichols

Although faculty might accept John Henry Cardinal Newman's reflection that real education takes place in the dining hall, few connect this statement to general education. General education is too often associated solely with the curriculum, the substance of education and the province of the faculty, while what happens in the dining hall is assumed to be extraneous to subject matter and the responsibility of the student affairs office.

This kind of separatism has been accentuated in recent decades by two developments. First, faculty backed off from their earlier concern for shaping the character of students and concentrated their full attention on the scholarly matters of teaching and research. Simultaneously, a new group of academic professionals was created to be responsible for the non-academic portions of student life, such as housing, admissions, health, counseling, and campus activities. In this fashion colleges and universities sought to provide students with services from a range of professionally trained individuals in both academic and student affairs. Not surprisingly, two separate administrative units were created at most institutions to supervise these twin functions.

Cross *(1976, p. 140) has cast a critical eye on this prevailing situation and declared:

> At best, this division of labor represents an administrative convenience; at worst, it depicts an erroneous and even dangerous conception of education in which values and attitudes are considered affective education—as though human values were devoid of intellectual analysis—while the study of physics is considered cognitive education—as though the development of humane and compassionate use of scientific knowledge were irrelevant to its possessor.

She found this situation a curious anomaly:

*May be found in Basic Readings, Chapter 2.

After all the years spent in academe analyzing the fallacy of various forms of dualism, it is ironic that we should find ourselves practicing cognitive-affective dualism in education. We have created separate (and not quite equal) structures to handle a dualistic conception of education. The vice president for student affairs is generally assigned responsibility for the out-of-class education of students, while the vice president for academic affairs deals with in-class education. Student personnel staff presumably have more expertise in affective education, whereas academic personnel are experts in cognitive education. (p. 139)

Since general education is distinctly holistic in nature and specifically includes attitudinal and value purposes as well as intellectual ones, it is important that this conventional form of dualistic thinking be transcended. One of the purposes of this chapter is to stress that there are non-curricular dimensions of general education.

A basic reason why non-curricular aspects may have been neglected is that so much that happens outside of the classroom seems to be the result of chance factors that cannot be controlled. To continue with Newman's example, if dinner conversation is educationally important, it is not at all clear with whom one will be eating or the directions the conversation may take. However, enough has been learned that the personal development of students can be taken out of the realm of accidental benefits of college and placed in the deliberate educational program. More attention can and should be given to creating the conditions outside the class which facilitate many of the goals of general education. A second purpose of this chapter is to indicate what some of these conditions might be. Finally, specific suggestions for enhancing the general education of students by non-curricular means will be offered.

A great deal of research has been conducted, mostly by behavioral scientists, on the growth and development of students, how they change during the college years, and which conditions facilitate these changes. Much of this research was stimulated by a publication entitled *Changing Values in College* (Jacob, 1957). This summary of the available literature yielded "...evidence that the quality of teaching has relatively little effect on the value outcomes of general eduation...so far as the great mass of students is concerned." (p. 7) The added proviso that "..._some_ teachers do exert a profound influence on _some_ students..." did little to modify the main thrust of its conclusions, which contradicted conventional wisdom about the educational value of teachers and the curriculum.

Enough new research was done so that one decade later Feldman and Newcomb were able to synthesize almost 1,500 studies in their book *The Impact of College on Students* (1969). Their final chapter consists of several findings, five of which are important to this topic:

Freshman-to-senior changes in several characteristics have been occurring with considerable uniformity in most American colleges and universities in recent decades. (p. 326)

Within the same college, experiences associated with the pursuit of different academic majors typically have effects over and

71

beyond those that can be accounted for by initial selection into those major fields. (p. 329)

Though faculty members are often individually influential, particularly in respect to career decisions, college faculties do not appear to be responsible for campus-wide impact except in settings where influence of student peers and of faculty complement and reinforce one another. (p. 330)

The conditions for campus-wide impacts appear to have been most frequently provided in small, residential, four-year colleges. These conditions probably include relative homogeneity of both faculty and student body together with opportunity for continuing interaction, not exclusively formal, among students and between students and faculty. (p. 331)

Attitudes held by students on leaving college tend to persist thereafter. (p. 332)

What changes in students consistently occur? The following characteristics tend to increase in college students on a freshman-to-senior basis (Feldman and Newcomb, 1969; Bowen, 1977): relativism, liberalism, open-mindedness, awareness of complexity, tolerance for ambiguity, aesthetic interests, cultural interests, intellectual interests, autonomy, personal identity, flexibility, dominance, confidence, self-sufficiency, ascendancy, assertiveness, readiness to express impulses, and positive self-image. The following qualities tend to decrease: moralism, religious preference, authoritarianism, dogmatism, ethnocentrism, prejudice, material interests, conservatism, deference, submissiveness, dependency, and stereotypical behavior. Obviously, not each individual student changes in all these ways, nor do students in any particular college, but these are changes which students, on the average, experience in a variety of schools.

There is a noteworthy tone of confidence conveyed by these authors. Even though the arguments are inductive, so that individual studies and lines of research establish conclusions only with some degree of probability, what impresses the summarizers and the synthesizers is the consistency of the findings. There is a marked convergence of independent lines of research about student development in college.

Although many of these changes are in the personal, social, and emotional realms, other studies demonstrate the importance of these matters for intellectual and ethical development. Perry (1970) describes developmental changes in students' assumptions about knowledge and values. As was mentioned in Chapter 4, he found that students progress through several intellectual stages from dualism to higher stages of development which permit more sophisticated intellectual and ethical analyses and judgments. Naturally, the transition from lower to higher intellectual stages may be accompanied by feelings of disillusionment, despair, rebellion, and other emotional and/or social analogs as firm belief systems crumble in the light of new knowledge. Indeed, personal development goes hand in hand with intellectual development, according to Perry and other behavioral theorists.

Chickering *(1969) has attempted to move the research findings a few steps in the direction of program design and implementation by identifying several conditions which accelerate or retard student development toward the objectives of general education. The major conditions are in six areas: clarity and consistency of educational objectives; institutional size; curriculum, teaching, and evaluation (grading); residence hall arrangements; faculty and administration; and student culture.

The challenge that Chickering poses to those involved in higher education is not that college should make a difference in the lives of young adults; that, it clearly does. "The basic argument of this book is that college can make a much *greater* difference. It can make a difference to more students and can make more of a difference to those reached" (p. 322). The task simply is to redesign structures and programs in ways that research has shown produce more impact. Each of the above non-curricular dimensions may be considered further.

Clarity and consistency of objectives, taken seriously, can strengthen institutional impact in three ways: a) there is greater internal consistency so that one element in an institution does not run counter to others; b) students are encouraged to make explicit their own purposes and to achieve them; and c) value commitments are brought into the open in such a context, so they then can be challenged, critiqued, and enhanced. Feldman and Newcomb (1969) cite three factors that affect consistency of objectives.

> *Student selection*—Admitting a large proportion of students who know and agree with the goals and purposes of the college puts the institution in a favorable position. This seems to make a big difference for both intellectual and values development. (p. 263)

> *Faculty goals and consensus*—The more the faculty agree on objectives, the more the student will be drawn into subcultures that harmonize with these objectives. The degree to which faculty, as distinct from administration and trustees, have the control and autonomy to implement their goal strategies is most relevant to the effectiveness of the institution. (p. 265)

> *Extracurricular activities and student organizations*—Some of these activities promote student development along desired lines and others detract from it. The institution must decide which are which, in terms of its goals and purposes, but it is essential that students be involved in making those decisions. (p 266)

Institutional size has been stressed by Smith and Bernstein (1979) as an important contributor to educational quality. It is not just that large institutions are impersonal and bureaucratic, for many small ones are also afflicted with those same problems. It is that large institutions provide proportionately fewer opportunities for students to obtain growth-producing experiences. Feldman and Newcomb (1969) conclude that total size of the institution would not be so important if there were smaller functional groupings in which students could learn and grow and derive mutual stimulation and support.

> The conditions that favor mutual stimulation and support must be described in interpersonal terms. They include, particularly, opportunity for continued interaction among the same individuals, allowing occasions for the discovery of mutual con-

geniality, preferably in varied settings—not just academic or just recreational or just residential, for example. (p. 337)

Even simple arrangements for interaction can have substantial impact. Faculty offices can be set up in dormitories or in a student center. Lounges and snack bars where members of the campus community may run into one another on an informal basis is another tested and fruitful approach. Or faculty may be encouraged to eat in student dining halls by subsidized pricing arrangements. Classes can be held in dormitories, or fireside chats by faculty, alumni, and administrators can be organized. Other ideas include academic and avocational clubs or college-subsidized events for students in educators' homes. More ambitious undertakings may include leadership programs for students, a system for official and frequent academic counseling, career exploration workshops, or arrangements for academic professionals to serve as mentors for students.

The importance and the impact of the residence experience have received their best documentation in Chickering (1974). He found that resident students are more advanced developmentally than commuter students at the time of entering college, and that these differences not only persist but are accentuated by the college experience, with students who live off-campus but not at home ranking closer to the commuters on most items. For instance, at the end of the freshman year, residents are more liberal in attitude, less concerned with mere financial survival, and more oriented to artistic creativity, social contribution, and political involvement. Commuters, on the other hand, are less satisfied with college, have lower self-esteem and a poorer self-image, and experience some diminution of their commitment to long-range goals. It is no surprise, then, that their drop-out rate is higher than the residents.

By the end of the four years of college, Chickering finds that commuters show remarkable differences from residents, particularly with regard to self-perceptions.

On six of eight skills—academic, writing, artistic, public speaking, leadership, athletic—dormitory students rate themselves higher than...commuters. On five of the skills—academic, writing, public speaking, leadership, athletic—students who live at home rank themselves lowest. (p. 74)

Various attempts at a causal analysis of these findings conclude that the diversity of experience, the challenge of interpersonal relations in the dormitory, and the fuller range of academic and extracurricular opportunities available to residents result in substantial advantages for educational outcomes and personal development.

The other side of the picture, of course, are the *dis*advantages of the commuting student:

Perhaps the most striking thing about these diverse studies is the consistency of the results. Whatever the institution, whatever the data, whatever the methods of analyses, the findings are the same. Students who live at home with their parents fall short of the kinds of learning and personal development typically desired by the institutions they attend and which might reasonably be expected when their special backgrounds are taken into account. (p. 84)

Taking both sides into consideration, there are two conclusions that emerge very clearly. One of them is summarized in the subtitle of *Commuting Versus Resident Students: Overcoming the Educational Inequities of Living Off Campus,* which implies that various types of short-term or quasi-residential experiences, such as workshops, retreats or trips, should be built into the college programs of commuters so that some of their disadvantages may be eliminated. The second conclusion goes back to Chickering's earlier work, *Education and Identity* (1969), namely, that residence in a college dormitory has great impact on the lives of young adults and that it can have even greater and broader impact if colleges work and design conditions so that what happens outside of class is consistent with the objectives of general education and with the curriculum.

It is important to note that the bulk of the studies that have been mentioned are a decade or so old and have been conducted on "traditional" 18-21 year-old students. There is little reason to expect that the results and their implications would not apply today for a similar population, but they are not directly applicable to such non-traditional students as older adults and part-timers. Many of these students do not live on campus and do not engage in the usual college activities that have been shown to be educationally valuable. New ways to involve these students in growth-producing experiences beyond the classroom have yet to be devised. They might consist of relating classroom learning to a student's job or family, helping a student to conceptualize and integrate life experiences, or giving him new experiences that challenge old values and opinions.

One of the principal obstacles to faculty influence on student development is lack of contact with students. A study (Underwood, 1968) done at the University of California, for instance, found that 75 percent of the freshmen and 63 percent of the seniors indicated that there was no faculty member whom they felt was particularly responsible to or for them. Quite a bit worse than that, "30 percent of the seniors...felt that very few or no faculty members were really interested in students." Four conditions on which faculty influence on student development seem to depend are: accessibility—especially establishing a warm and informal stance; authenticity—faculty with firm and well-integrated systems of values and behaviors; knowledge—including both competence in one's field and acquaintance with students' backgrounds; and ability to talk with and to listen to students (Wilson, et al., 1975).

The power of the college culture, particularly the peer group, has been noted by several individuals. On the presupposition that "the total environment of the student is educational," Miller and Prince (1976, p. 4) survey the literature in the field of student affairs work and derive five facets that characterize the ideal developmental milieu: (1) the various elements in it must serve common institutional goals; (2) there must be a purposeful relationship between formal learning and the student's growth outside the classroom; (3) a reasonable degree of compatibility between an individual and the college is necessary to promote maximum growth; (4) there must be a true relationship between what occurs on the campus and what happens in the "real world"; and (5) an effective milieu responds to the developmental needs of its inhabitants in terms of stimulation, security, order, freedom, and life space. Student subgroups are not "invariably supportive of, nor necessarily opposed to, the intellectual values of the faculty," as noted by Feldman and Newcomb (p. 263). Such groupings are neither automatically in favor of nor inimical to the broader range of institutional objectives. But their attitudes, values, and expectations can either support or undermine a general education curriculum. Steps can be taken to infuse the student peer culture with the values embodied in the curriculum.

It may be noted that several institutions have taken action to improve the educational environment for different groups of students. A number of institutions have created deliberate living-learning environments or entire sub-colleges, typically offering a more integrated curriculum and closer student-faculty relationships. The 1960's saw much attention to such experimental contexts; some of these have been closed (e.g., Bensalem at Fordham University); others have been transformed into educational brokering centers for adults (Justin Morrill at Michigan State University); and others have become institutionalized (The Paracollege at St. Olaf College). For adults there have been weekend colleges, such as that operated by Mundelein College, and short-term residency programs as offered by Goddard College. "Least restricted environments" for the handicapped at schools like Hofstra University and St. Andrews Presbyterian College represent other approaches to enhance the environment, especially for nontraditional students.

A final factor that may be stressed is the importance of experiences beyond the campus. Experiential learning whether through field studies, domestic or foreign travel, internships, or community action projects can be important learning experiences for students. Student volunteer programs, some of which operate under the leadership of the federal ACTION agency, provide many learning opportunities through what are being called service-learning centers. Although some of these experiences may be granted academic credit and hence be a part of the formal curriculum, it seems to be more important that students have such experiences than that they receive academic credit for them.

Astin (1977) has reviewed the conditions that are most effective in promoting student growth in the direction of general education objectives, and issued a stinging critique of major academic policies. He concludes that recent public policies have moved in directions opposite from those which would promote student development as documented by the research literature. The expansion of the public sector, the decline of single-sex colleges, the proliferation of public community colleges, the deemphasis of the residential experience, open admissions, and the denigration of grade point averages are decried because each decreases the educational impact of colleges and universities. Of course, many of these policies were made to achieve other purposes, notably the expansion of access to a college education for larger numbers of persons.

A different approach is to utilize this body of knowledge to devise programs and activities that promote the goals of general education. Faculty, student affairs professionals, and other administrators can work together with students to assure that all facets of the college community contribute in a conscious and deliberate way to student development. Several possibilities for collaboration have been suggested by Katz (1979): jointly led activities (student government, social events, clubs); jointly taught courses (leadership training, interpersonal skills, career preparation, training of peer counselors); joint research (student characteristics, subcultures, growth); and faculty workshops by student affairs professionals (residence education in general, counseling skills, academic impact on dormitory life, programs for commuters outside the classroom).

Katz also proposes a plan of implementation for this collaboration. One may start by choosing a few key faculty who can collaborate with student affairs people and encouraging these faculty members to enlist the aid of others when needed. Katz recommends that the administration maintain a low profile during such efforts and provide encouragement and facilitation by offering released time, secretarial help, and a modest budget for operations rather than monetary rewards. This guarantees that the enthusiasm generated by and invested in the project comes from personal commitment to its aims and gives a higher level of assurance that the operation will be maintained.

Of course there are many other possibilities. Student activities, student affairs programs, cultural and intellectual events, experiential learning activities in the surrounding community, advising and counseling, informal conversations, and externships/internships are all potential contributors to student development. Each can be harnessed to serve the ends of general education.

General education, then, does involve non-curricular dimensions. There are several conditions that can be manipulated deliberately to enhance the personal and intellectual growth of students, and a number of specific steps can be undertaken at any school interested in doing so. A holistic plan for college education involves not only the integration of curricular elements, such as general education and a major concentration, but also the integration of the curriculum and non-curriculum. Faculty members and student affairs staff are all educators who need to work together to fashion coherent educational programs. Congruence between curricular and extra-curricular experiences, and between both of these and the mission of the college, is the context which research shows to be the most favorable for student development.

## ANNOTATED BIBLIOGRAPHY

Appleton, J., Moore, P., and Vinton, J. "A Model for the Effective Delivery of Student Services in Academic Schools and Departments." *Journal of Higher Education,* July/August, 1978, pp. 372-81.
> Student services such as housing, financial aid, job placement and career development, health and counseling services grew rapidly after World War II and for the most part were administered separately from academic affairs. A new model of organization is described in which each academic unit identifies student affairs personnel whose work is coordinated by the vice present for student affairs. This decentralized approach helps the student affairs division with its personnel to become a more effective resource for academic units, which in turn give more attention to working directly with students.

Astin, A., *Four Critical Years.* San Francisco: Jossey-Bass, 1977.
> Beginning in 1966, the Cooperative Institutional Research Program studied the impact of college on over 200,000 students from 300 institutions. Astin not only presents the findings from that study but discusses the policy implications of these findings. The tables used to present data are excellent.

Bowen, H. *Investment in Learning: The Individual and Social Value of American Higher Education.* San Francisco: Jossey-Bass, 1977.

Surveys an extensive range of literature including works by psychologists, philosophers, historians, educators, sociologists, economists, and critics. Outcomes for individuals are examined for cognitive learning, emotional and moral development, citizenship, economic productivity, family life, consumer behavior, leisure, and health. The consequences for society are seen in terms of research and scholarship, public service, public policy analyses, cultivation of creative literature and fine arts, and economic returns. The author concludes that higher education is well worth its cost.

Chickering, A. *Commuting Versus Resident Students.* San Francisco: Jossey-Bass, 1974.

This text is a bit heavier on persuasive discourse than the preceding ones, but the case is very well argued. There is a gap between commuters and residents to begin with, and the different college experiences they have serve to widen that gap. Whereas Astin (above) attacks the government policies that promote heavier emphasis on commuter colleges, Chickering is more concerned with suggesting how the inequities between the two groups might be overcome by simulating the residence experience for commuters.

Committee on the Student in Higher Education. *The Student in Higher Education.* New Haven, Conn.: The Hazen Foundation, 1968.

This is a short, readable report that takes a holistic view of education. Although dated, its ideas remain contemporary. "[The student's] interaction with teachers, his encounter with the social structure of the college administration, the friendship groups in which he becomes integrated, the values he acquires from student culture, the atmosphere of flexibility or rigidity which permeates the school environment, the playfulness or the seriousness, the 'practicality' or the 'spontaneity' of operative educational goals of his college—all of these have an immense, if not yet precisely measured, impact. . .on students."

Donnellan, M. and Ebben, J. *Values Pedagogy in Higher Education.* Adrian, Mich.: Siena Heights College, 1978.

This text is the proceedings of a conference on values pedagogy on the postsecondary level held at Siena Heights in April, 1978. It is included because more than half of the 17 presentations were detailed illustrations of what various colleges were trying to do to work at student development in ways more holistic than is usual.

Feldman, A. and Newcomb, T. *The Impact of College on Students.* San Francisco: Jossey-Bass, 1969.

This work is a classic. It brings together the results of nearly 1500 studies of higher education over the 40 years from 1929 to 1969. Volume I is the text with the authors' interpretations of the data classified according to different aspects of college life, a synthesis in the concluding chapter, and 76 pages of references. Volume II contains tables summarizing the results of the studies they incorporated into their text.

Fisch, L. "Student-Faculty Relations: Bridging the Gap." *NASPA Journal,* Spring, 1978, pp. 40-45.

Although brief, the article contains suggestions for activities to improve student-faculty relationships categorized under educational programs, social programs, and programs in which faculty take on student personnel functions.

Katz, J. "Collaboration of Academic Faculty and Student Affairs Professionals for Student Development." In D. Tilley, L. Benezet, J. Katz, and W. Shanteau, *The Student Affairs Dean and the President: Trends in Higher Education.* Ann Arbor, Michigan: ERIC Counseling & Personnel Sources Clearinghouse, 1979, 33-54.

This paper articulates the basic ideas in the concept of holistic student development and indicates how the whole personality is involved in academic learning. Several practical suggestions for collaboration in such arenas as professional seminars, student-faculty dynamics in the classroom, joint teaching, research on education, advising, career exploration, counseling, residences, and student peer relations.

Katz, J. and Associates. *No Time for Youth: Growth and Constraint in College Students.* San Francisco: Jossey-Bass, 1968.

Reports on a study of 3,500 Berkeley and Stanford students during their college years. Discusses the varying ways students cope with the myriad aspects of college life and makes recommendations for improvements in teaching, the curriculum, and other areas.

Katz, J., ed. "Services for Students." *New Directions for Higher Education* 3, San Francisco: Jossey-Bass, Autumn, 1973.

A series of articles which emphasizes practical new ways to plan and organize a wide range of services for students. Chapters deal with university housing, efforts to link residence halls with the classroom, and psychiatric services, as well as advising.

Miller, T. and Prince, J. *The Future of Student Affairs.* San Francisco: Jossey-Bass, 1976.

This book is valuable for examining collaboration between faculty and student affairs personnel. It's a practical book, full of experience and suggestive ways of doing things. There is a list of references, but of even more value are the pages of model programs and contact persons at institutions which are on the way to achieving a well-integrated program of student development.

Moos, R. *Evaluating Educational Environments.* San Francisco: Jossey-Bass, 1979.

The specific focus of this research is to discover which factors in classroom and living arrangements have a facilitative, and which ones have an inhibiting impact on students. Moos provides the full text of his questionnaires as well as guidelines for using them.

O'Banion, T. "Exceptional Practices in Community Junior College Student Personnel Programs." In T. O'Banion and A. Thurston, eds., *Student Development Programs in the Community Junior College.* Englewood Cliffs, N.J.: Prentice-Hall, 1972, pp. 180-93.

A discussion of several programs in the areas of organization and administration of services, academic advising, individual and group counseling, student activities, and orientation. Other chapters of the book are useful.

Pascarella, E., Terenzini, P., and Hibel, J. "Student-Faculty Interactional Settings and Their Relationship to Predicted Academic Performance." *Journal of Higher Education,* September-October, 1978, pp. 450-63.

Investigators found that student-faculty interaction, particularly that focusing on intellectual and career concerns, influenced academic achievement, even after controlling for 12 entering characteristics. Taken together with their earlier findings that such interaction affected student persistence, the authors conclude that "nonclassroom settings are particularly rich in their potentialities for faculty influence on student attitudes, values, and, perhaps, even behaviors." They suggest that educational policies concerning space and facilities should reflect these facts.

Sanford, N., ed. *The American College.* New York: John Wiley, 1962.

A massive classic work that deals with nearly all aspects of college life, particularly as they impinge on the students. Chapters deal with such diverse topics as motivation in college attendance, characteristics of students in different types of schools and fields of study, the college environment, and dropouts.

Smith, V. and Bernstein, A. *The Impersonal Campus.* San Francisco: Jossey-Bass. 1979.

An analysis of the impact of size on the quality of education at colleges and universities. Contains suggestions by which small colleges can extend the range of their curricular offerings and learning programs by means of specialized consortia and cooperative arrangements with community groups. Also has useful ideas about how large institutions can overcome impersonality, by way of cluster colleges, block scheduling of courses, decentralization of student services, theme houses, and programs tailored to specific groups of students. Specific examples are provided.

Snyder, B. *The Hidden Curriculum.* New York: Knopf, 1971.

Argues that the formal course curriculum is only one, and often not the most influential, form of curriculum. The standards, norms, and expectations of the college, the peer group, and the faculty constitute a powerful "hidden curriculum" that plays a major role in shaping students' educational experiences.

Wilson, R., Gaff, J., Dienst, E., Wood, L., and Baury, L. *College Professors and Their Impact on Students.* New York: John Wiley, 1975.

The results of two surveys are reported. The first discusses faculty views of the importance of teaching, classroom teaching styles, attitudes toward change, and related matters. The second relates faculty teaching styles and relationships with students to the development of students during the four years of college. Factors involved in facilitating intellectual development and other kinds of growth are identified.

# ADDITIONAL BIBLIOGRAPHY

Armentrout, W. "Neglected Values in Higher Education: Needed Reorganization in Curricular and Extra-Curricular Activities to Provide Significant Experiences." *Journal of Higher Education*, July-August, 1979, pp. 361-67.

Becker, H., Geer, B., Hughes, E., and Strauss, A. *Boys in White: Student Culture in Medical School.* Chicago: University of Chicago Press, 1961.

Berman, W. "Student Activities and Student Development." *NASPA Journal*, Autumn, 1978, pp. 52-54.

Catterall, C. and Gazda, G. *Strategies for Helping Students.* Springfield, Illinois: Thomas, 1978.

Clark, B., Heist, P., McConnell, T., Trow, M., and Yonge, G. *Students and College: Interaction and Change.* Berkeley, California: Center for Research and Development in Higher Education, University of California, 1972.

Decoster, D. and Mable, P., eds. *Student Development and Education in College Residence Halls.* Washington, D.C.: American College Personnel Association, 1974.

Harrington, T. *Student Personnel Work in Urban Colleges.* New York: Intext, 1969.

Healy, C. *Career Counseling in the Community College.* Springfield, Illinois: Thomas, 1974.

Jacob, P. *Changing Values in College.* New York: Harper, 1957.

Jennings, S. "Academic Advising in the Residence Halls." *NASPA Journal*, Autumn, 1978, pp. 55-60.

McDaniel, T. "The Cognitive and Affective in Liberal Education: Can We Have Both?" *Liberal Education*, October, 1979, pp. 465-71.

Newcomb, T. and Wilson, E. *College Peer Groups: Problems and Prospects for Research.* Chicago: Aldine, 1966.

Perry, W. *Forms of Intellectual and Ethical Development in the College Years.* New York: Holt, Rinehart & Winston, 1970.

*The Idea Handbook for Colleges and Universities.* Academy for Educational Development, 1414 22nd Street, N.W., Washington, D.C. 20037, 1979.

Wallace, D. "A Comparative Analysis of the Needs of Undergraduate Adults." *NASPA Journal*, Winter, 1979, pp. 15-23.

# PROGRAMS FOR NON-CURRICULAR DIMENSIONS

Bethel College
North Newton, Kansas 67117
Walter Friesen, Vice President

This small Mennonite college attempted to strengthen itself by designing its curriculum and governance around a unifying theme based on its historical commitments. Peace studies is that theme which has been carried through in all aspects of the college.

College of Charleston
Charleston, South Carolina 29401
Career Development Office
Frank Van Aalst, Dean of Career Development

A comprehensive program is established including cooperatives (full-time work for six months), internships (part-time work in career-related positions), and volunteer service in area agencies. In addition, the program conducts career planning workshops, a career information center, "career tests" featuring various occupations, "venturing" activities (in which students go to employers), and placement.

Luzerne County Community College
Nanticoke, Pennsylvania 18634
Patrick Santacroce, Director, Special Programs

Luzerne's "Operation-GO " program is designed to provide personalized counseling, tutorial, instruction, and cultural activities in support of disadvantaged students.

Michigan State University
East Lansing, Michigan 48824
Service Learning Center
Jane S. Smith, Director

The Center develops placements for students in community programs such as corrections, education, government, social services, and health. Volunteer programs are designed to link the students' educational interests and work experience needs. Although the Center does not award credit, it does develop placements for students enrolled in academic study in addition to providing placements for career exploration, skill enrichment, and personal enrichment.

National Association of Student Personnel Administrators
Portland State University
P.O. Box 751
Portland, Oregon 97207
Channing M. Briggs, Executive Director

This organization primarily serves student affairs staff members and deals with a number of issues concerning the full range of student development. Activities include an annual conference, regional conferences and workshops, publication of a journal and monographs, and other specific activities, such as an institute for academic and student affairs personnel.

National Society for Internships and Experiential Education
1735 I Street, N.W., Suite 601
Washington, D.C. 20006
Jane Kendall, Associate Executive Director

This national membership-based organization compiles and publishes three major directories on experiential learning, two of which focus on undergraduate education. Of the two undergraduate directories, one covers internships on a national scope while the other concentrates on the Washington, D.C. area. The directories stress quality internships which are categorized by fields such as fine arts, history, business and management, etc. The Society also publishes a bi-monthly newsletter which serves as a source of information on experiential education and is available to members. Among other relevant topics, the newsletter stresses funding, legislation, program development, and research and evaluation.

National Student Educational Fund
2000 P Street, N.W., Suite 305
Washington, D.C. 20036
Karon Cox, President

This organization serves as a pipeline for several projects concerned with higher education from a student's perspective. It recently awarded prizes for student productions that conveyed to their peers what aspects of the college experience are like, including financial aid, health care, evaluation of teaching, and prevention of rape.

Saint Joseph's College
Rensselaer, Indiana 47978
The Core Curriculum
John Nichols, Coordinator

The College attempts to have an impact on student peer groups and residence halls by means of a common academic experience for all students and about 60% of the faculty.

University of Alabama
The New College
University, Alabama 35486
Bernie Sloan, Dean

The New College represents a very successful project in setting up learning communities within the context of a large university. A wide variety of students are selected for the College, and faculty come from a diversity of disciplines. They engage in the interdisciplinary courses at the College.

University of California
Santa Cruz, California 95064
Oakes College
J. Herman Blake, Provost

Oakes, one of eight cluster colleges, has a commitment both to minority education and to maximizing the benefits of informal education. Half of the faculty and 40 percent of the students are minority, and heavy emphasis is placed on natural sciences, computers, innovative teaching methods, counseling, and informal interaction beyond the classroom.

University of Michigan
Ann Arbor, Michigan 48109
Center for Helping Organizations Improve Choice in Education
School of Education
Joan S. Stark, Director

Project CHOICE is working with 19 colleges and universities that are revising their printed materials providing more accurate, comprehensive and useable information to prospective students. CHOICE is using this experience to develop models of better information and to identify successful procedures for information improvement that can serve as models for other institutions. CHOICE is also conducting research on the role of printed information in student college choice. Workshops for individuals from other institutions, a clearinghouse on student consumer information, and a national Linking Service of consultants on better information issues are other activities.

University of Michigan
Ann Arbor, Michigan 48109
Residential College
John Mersereau, Director

The residential college, established in 1967 at the University of Michigan, is a four-year degree granting program in the College of Literature, Science and the Arts (LSA). In a world-stature university, the small college atmosphere encourages students to become actively involved in the pursuit of a liberal arts education in the study of humanities, natural and social sciences. In this living/learning environment, the student has easy access to a quality faculty who combine professional expertise in the field with concern for the students' development and growth.

University of South Carolina
Columbia, South Carolina 29208
University 101
John Gardner, Director

The University has several years' experience with a program to orient freshmen to handle a university environment and to provide a support group by which to acclimate themselves to that environment. University 101 is a three-credit hour freshman course taught by faculty and professional staff.

# 7. Teaching and Advising in General Education

## by Judith A. Redwine

The topics of teaching and advising seldom figure prominently in discussions of general education. Philosophical concepts, qualities of an educated man or women, and curricular models are given such a central place in the contemporary debate over general education that other crucial topics are given short shrift. Yet with only a moment's reflection one will recognize that any curriculum is only as good as the effectiveness with which the courses are taught and the quality of advice which students receive. In fact, general education probably contains examples of the best and the worst of both teaching and advising.

The acts of teaching and advising have been compared by Mayhew (1969).

> The act of teaching is an act of forming and creating. Even though the teacher may adopt relatively passive means, he is likely to have certain objectives that he wishes to achieve. Advising, on the other hand, is much more concerned with facilitating the evolution of goals and solutions to problems of students themselves. Where the teacher injects his personality, the advisor needs to subdue his own impact as a person. In the classroom, a subject external to the student is important to the teaching equation; but the student himself is the subject in an advising relationship. In teaching, teacher responses tend to be less subtle than is demanded in the intimate, face-to-face advising function. (p. 172)

These differences makes separate treatments appropriate, beginning with a consideration of teaching and general education.

### TEACHING

Teaching has been defined as an art (Highet, 1950), a craft (Eble, 1976), manipulation of the variables of instruction to achieve intended learning (Wilson, Lopis, and Radke, 1978), an act of celebration (Phenix, 1975), and managing an instructional system (Banathy, 1978). If one is weary of definitions, Owen (1978) presents a list of delightful analogs including safari guide, priest, efficiency expert, and lover.

General education falls prey to a whole set of abuses and impediments that are common across undergraduate teaching. These include: faculty who lack preparation for teaching; preoccupation of the best qualified teachers with research and publication instead of teaching; an advancement system which rewards research and publications more than teaching; assignment of great portions of undergraduate instruction to the least experienced instructors and to graduate assistants; strong traditional acceptance of amateurism in college teaching; academic myths (e.g., good teachers are born not made, knowledge of a subject matter is synonymous with the ability to teach that subject); failure to obtain and use feedback; conservatism regarding change in teaching methods and styles; misuse of the concept of academic freedom resulting in a shield for incompetent teachers and administrators; and preoccupation with what is immediate and obvious rather than with what is important *(Cross, 1976; Dearing, 1970; Gaff, 1978).

In addition to these pervasive problems, others are specifically endemic to general education teaching. For one thing, general education courses are "nonmajor" and often lower level; consequently, they lack status within the academic pecking order. For both faculty and students, general education can become merely what one does while awaiting the opportunity to teach or take "real" courses in one's major area of interest. Just as one does not expect much from time spent in a doctor's waiting room since it is lost time anyway, expectations for general education teaching and learning are often low. Further, the fact that general education commonly is seen as the institutional breadwinner may result in an undue emphasis on efficiency in teaching. This drive to net a profit appears in the form of cost-effective teaching, i.e, very large classes conducted by frequently untrained and unsupervised graduate assistants or neophyte faculty members (Dearing, 1970). Also because of this supporting role, general education courses are sometimes seen as in the public domain. A teacher may feel duty-bound to cover the subject regardless of his interest or competence in portions of it; he may not feel free to tamper with general education courses with the same gay abandon possible in courses buried farther back on the private estates of the disciplines. Who knows or cares if auto-tutorial instruction is implemented in Advanced Psychology of Abnormal Behavior in Late Adolescence? Trying the same innovation in General Psychology, required of all freshmen, could cause reverberations all across a campus. Thus, the supporting role and common property characteristics of general education tend to limit the freedom of its teachers, diminish their enthusiasm, and predispose uninspired performances.

The third challenge for general education teaching centers on the nature of the students. Faculty members have complained that many are ill-prepared, career-oriented, and not particularly interested in general education courses. As was discussed in Chapter 4, there is an increase in the number of non-traditional students with needs, interests, and learning styles that differ in important ways from students in the past. The literature is

---

*May be found in Basic Readings, Chapter 2.

unanimous in recognizing the need for a broad variety of teaching styles and methods to match this full spectrum of student attitudes, abilities, and readiness. But competence across a broad variety of teaching strategies is only the beginning; the general education teacher must attempt to match these with collective and individual student needs. Teachers who continue to be "...absurdly vain about their innocence of any formal instruction in curriculum design, testing techniques, and formal classroom procedures" (Dearing, 1970, p. 222-23) may be a hit in the faculty lounge, but they are apt to be eaten alive in general education classes.

A fourth difficulty encountered when teaching in general education is related to the lack of understanding of the concept of general or liberal education on the part of both faculty and students. The chapter "General Education: An Idea in Distress" in *Missions of the College Curriculum (Carnegie Foundation for the Advancement of Teaching, 1977), provides background for understanding this problem. More specifically, Averill (1970) and Gaff (1978) discuss the inadequacy of preparation of college teachers for general education teaching. Consequently, little attention has been paid to the teaching skills required to transform a hodge-podge of distribution requirements into a holistic liberal education that is more than the sum of separate courses.

Finally, when attempts are made to improve teaching in general education, they have all the risks, complexities, problems, and political overtones involved in any experimental program. For personal descriptions of what it is like to be involved in an experimental program, see MacDonald's *Five Experimental Colleges* (1972).

Despite the existence of these problems, the literature contains some promising prospects concerning teaching in general education. Several positive current trends may be identified. The first trend includes all those teaching improvements which are based upon the recognition that the teacher is the director, rather than the star performer, of *all* the variables in the instructional setting. As the person responsible for arranging students' learning experiences, the instructor chooses from among many combinations in order to provide the best possible situation for learning. Possible combinations include variations in group size, mode of delivery, degree of teacher control, approach to the discipline, and amount of classroom interaction. Obviously, this view of teaching forces one out of the sole use of the traditional lecture approach.

A second encouraging tendency is the experimentation with a large number of instructional methods, many of them recent developments. Descriptions of various instructional methods are provided by Kozma, Belle, and Williams (1978). Techniques include one-way media, such as the lecture, book, instructional television, motion pictures, still projection media, and audio procedures; two-way media, including discussion, role playing, simulation, and games; and several self-instructional media. Advantages and disadvantages, appropriate uses, and practical tips are discussed for each technique. Brown and Thornton (1971) and McKeachie and Kulik (1975) are also useful resources. Clearly there are now opportunities to go beyond conventional lecture and seminar teaching in general education and to incorporate many of these instructional techniques in such courses.

Another set of promising possibilities for teaching concerns the application of systems theory to general education teaching. Systems theory, developed during World War II and widely used by business and industry, has more recently begun to influence education. Banathy's *Instructional Systems* (1968) provides an excellent introduction to the concepts, principles and applications of systems theory in education. Evidence of the influence of systems theory on general education includes: emphasis on outcome objectives (MacMillan, 1975; Davis, 1977) or competence (Grant, et al., 1979) in design of curriculum, conceptualization of teaching as designing and managing an instructional system (Bligh, 1975; Davis, 1977; Kozma, 1977; Nash, 1975), and the use of evaluative feedback to adjust teaching practices (Dressel, 1976; Millar, 1974).

The recognition of the possiblities for synergism in group teaching represents a fourth approach. Rather than viewing instruction as a series of solitary acts, teachers in some general education progams work together. A team of teachers, for example, can better achieve certain purposes than just one teacher, and looking at a problem from the perspective of several disciplines can be more valuable than looking at the same problem from the vantage point of just one discipline. Team and/or interdisciplinary teaching may involve special skills, such as the ability to range beyond familiar disciplinary categories, interest in learning new content, willingness to share classroom authority, and tolerance for different pedagogical and personal styles. There seems to be a growing awareness among general education teachers of the wisdom of avoiding "turnstyle" teaching as opposed to "team" teaching and competition rather than cooperation among the individuals and disciplines.

Another set of possible improvements in general education teaching reflects a shift in focus from the teacher to the student. The results of this concern for the student are manifested in: concern for instructor-student relationship (Rogers, 1969); stress on the student as a whole person (Axelrod, 1973); looking at teaching from students' perspectives (Ericksen, 1974); increase in student involvement and responsibility in the learning process (Dressel and Thompson, 1970; Milton, 1978); more individualization (Boylan, 1977; Toft, 1974); recognition of special needs of older (Milton, 1978) and "new" students (Cross, 1971; Ognibene, 1975); greater awareness of and concern for consistency among student learning style, level of development, and instructor's method of teaching (Fiella, 1975; Glaser, 1968; Milton, 1972).

Still another set of prospects can be characterized as a recognition of the relationship between the *process* and the *product* of a general education. Simply stated, the literature reveals a growing awareness that students need opportunities to practice the behaviors of a liberal education *within* their general education experiences if they are to become liberally educated persons. These behaviors include the ability and skill to think logically, communicate clearly, and make moral judgments. This implies, then, that students must have opportunities to practice performing these same behaviors which, of course, then requires certain teaching methods (Abel, 1978; Rainsford, 1978). This approach encourages teaching methods which emphasize higher thinking skills of analysis, synthesis, and evaluation; questioning and inquiry strategies, individual and group problem solving, cogent written and oral communication, clarification of values, alignment of behaviors with values, and anticipation of consequences of values and decisions.

Finally, teaching in general education can benefit from the recent surge of interest in faculty development. Although faculty development has many facets, one emphasis it has had during the last few years is the improvement of teaching. Several excellent sources on faculty development exist. These include: *Faculty Development in a Time of Retrenchment* by the Group for Human Development in Higher Education (1974); Gaff and Justice (In Gaff, 1978); Bergquist, Phillips and Quehl, 1975, 1977; Centra, 1977; Gaff, 1975; Gaff, Festa, and Gaff, 1978; and Lindquist, 1978. Many colleges and universities have established centers for instructional development or for career enrichment of their faculties; some of them are involved in helping faculty to develop competency in general education teaching or to gain professional or personal renewal by working in the context of the general education program.

## ADVISING

Levine *(1978, p. 134) has defined advising as "counseling available to students or potential students that is directly or indirectly concerned with the undergraduate curriculum." After a brief history of advising, he describes the state of the art according to four major types of advising: academic, personal, career, and special group. Also included are descriptions and examples of sources of advising such as:

> ...books and pamphlets, college orientation, faculty members, freshmen seminars, administrators, professional counselors and counseling centers, students and team advising. Other forms of advising occasionally available to students include computers and other communication technology, alumni, community resource people, and brokerage organizations. (p. 140)

There is frequent use of specific examples of programs which allows for follow-up by the interested reader.

Chickering, in Katz's "Service for Students," *New Directions for Higher Education* (1973), states that college advising in the future must take into account three fundamental changes underway: increasingly diverse students, increasingly diverse educational options, and self-development as the emerging goal of education. Because of these changes, Chickering believes the role of the college advisor will become increasingly complex and critical as he assists in matching students' needs with educational opportunities. Mash (1978, p. 33) has urged also that a high priority be placed on advising in order to minimize "the discrepancy between the perceived importance of academic advising and the way it is performed on many campuses." his article also contains recommendations from the Carnegie Commission on Policy Studies in HIgher Education concerning greater emphasis on advising.

A review of the literature on advising indicates some deterrents to strong advising programs. These include general failure to acknowledge the importance of advising, with the obvious result that faculty are not rewarded for it (Biggs, et al., 1975). Related to this is an apparent need to clarify, and in some cases, increase student, faculty, and institutional expectations for advising. The contributions that successful programs make to a quality education must be recognized if the limited support for advising now available is to be retained or increased.

The nature of advising itself is problematic; that is, a certain element of voluntariness or spontaneity seems to be essential to effective advising. It is difficult to find a balance between providing the benefits of effective advising for all students without destroying this quality. In addition, a characteristic of effective advising is that it is holistic. Few individual advisors are prepared to deal with the whole student in an advising relationship, and when a student must deal with several specialized advisors something seems to get lost in the shuffle.

Just as general education teaching has some bright as well as bleak spots, advising in such a context shows some promise of improvement. There is a growing recognition of the importance of the person of the advisor (Parker, et al., 1976), understanding of the multiple skills of advising (Kopplin and Rice, 1975; NASPA Journal, 1977), and awareness of the importance of a suitable match between advisor and advisee. Advising workshops are advertised nationally in the *Chronicle of Higher Education;* how-to books exist (Hardee, 1970; Kramer and Gardner, 1977), and some general education programs, such as University College, Memphis State University, have included special training for advisors. Obviously, it is no longer assumed that every faculty member automatically is prepared to be an effective advisor.

The advising process is a vehicle to increase the awareness, understanding, and valuing of general education on the part of both advisors and advisees. It cannot be taken for granted that everyone understands the relationships between and among general education courses, much less perceives their value (Berdie, 1975; Faculty Involvement in Career and Academic Advisement, 1977; Kurlander, 1974; Morgan, 1977). But a sensitive and thoughtful discussion between students and advisors can help provide such an understanding.

The literature indicates that the role of advising is expanding to meet student needs more realistically. For example, a wide variety of delivery modes is in use, human as well as technological, e.g., television and computers. The range of topics in advising is broadening to include careers, personal development, study skills, and financial aid (Berdie, 1975; Biggs et al., 1975; "Faculty Involvement in Career and Academic Advisement," SREB, 1977; Groves and Kennedy, 1974; Kurlander, 1974; Morgan, 1977). A developmental approach which "should go well beyond the interpretation of degree requirements and course registration" is encouraged by Mash (1978, p. 34). The length of time advising is available to students is increasing by beginning advising earlier, often before the student enrolls. Other programs, such as Auburn University's Mentor program (PIRIT Newsletter, December, 1976), are designed to improve the quality of the time advisors and advisees spend together.

Special advising systems are being designed to meet the unique needs of certain students groups, such as women (Valencia Community College's Center for Continuing Education for Women, Orlando, Florida), adults (Sacred Heart University, Hartford, Conn.), and minorities (University of California, Santa Cruz). Levine *(1978) gives several examples of advising programs designed to help students whose needs are not shared by students generally.

As in teaching, systems theory has had a positive effect on advising. More attention is being paid to the total advising available to, or experienced by, students. The various components of the advising system and their interrelationships as well as the compatibility of the advising system within the overall system of all student services are being examined (Dameron and Wolf, 1974; "Faculty Involvement in Career and Academic Advisement," 1977; Field and Hecker, 1974; Hardee, 1970; Katz, 1973; Miller and Prince, 1976; NASPA Journal, 1977). Evaluation feedback from student clients of the advising systems can also be used to improve the system (Hardee, 1970; Stein and Spille, 1974).

The precise composition of the ideal advising system, the one most effective and economical, does not seem clear from the literature. However, persons interested in improving advising in general might consider the following:

> Providing early and continuous advising based upon thorough understanding of students' interest developed through effective pre-admission data collection (Mash, 1978);

> Emphasizing personal and vocational advising;

> Integrating advising services (Mayhew and Ford, 1971; University of Minnesota General College's HELP Center);

> Attending to requirements of such special student groups as academically disadvantaged or older students;

> Employing a wide variety of delivery modes, making certain that they form an integrated whole;

> Using the advising process to induce linkages among liberal learning, vocational possibilities, and social issues (Mentor Advising Project, Indiana University at South Bend);

> Making advising a part of each instructor's course load rather than a tacked-on assignment (Metropolitan State University);

> Encouraging faculty with strength in counseling to emphasize advising in their course loads (Mayhew and Ford, 1971);

> Initiating in-service sessions for faculty to keep them abreast of curricular developments outside their departments (Sterling College) and to develop skills of advising (Memphis State);

> Adopting faculty reward systems that encourage faculty efforts in advising (Sarah Lawrence College);

> Pairing faculty and students with similar expectations of the advising relationship.

Those who seek to improve the quality of general education cannot afford to ignore the twin factors of teaching and advising. They will have to face squarely those deep-seated academic factors that work against excellence in each of these areas and take advantage of the trends toward improvement. If successful, these efforts may not only aid general education, but also enhance the effectiveness of teaching and advising in other areas.

# ANNOTATED BIBLIOGRAPHY

Allen, D., Melnik, M., and Peele, C., eds. *Reform, Renewal, Reward*. Proceedings of the International Conference on Improving University Teaching, October 4-8, 1974. Amherst, Mass.: Clinic to Improve University Teaching, University of Massachusetts, Amherst 01002, 1975.

> An assortment of papers on teaching and its improvement. Major sections focus on the case for improving university teaching and some problems and questions to confront: teaching skills and behaviors, student roles, curriculum, educational technology, change strategies, international perspective, and rewarding teaching.

Axelrod, J. *The University Teacher as Artist*. San Francisco: Jossey-Bass, 1973.

> Poses provocatively the "aesthetics of teaching." Distinguishes between teacher-craftsmen, who seek excellence in didactic modes of teaching, and teacher-artists, who excel through evocative modes. Describes through rich portraits of individual teachers four aspects of evocative styles: mastery of facts and principles of a discipline, the professor as an authority, development of students' minds, and development of students as whole persons. Argues that teacher-artists are needed and points to educational reform that will support their development.

Berdie, R. "Counseling and Liberal Education." *Journal of College Student Personnel* 16, January, 1975, pp. 3-9.

> Maintains that counselors are too preoccupied with the personal and vocational aspects of student development; instead they should help students discover and develop their own educational philosophy and direct them to pay more attention to furthering their liberal education. Faculty advisors are concerned with the substance of education and should interrelate their concerns with those of the counselors.

Bergquist, W., Phillips, S., and Quehl, G. *A Handbook for Faculty Development*. Washington, D.C.: Council for the Advancement of Small Colleges, Vols. I and II. 1975 and 1977.

> These two volumes contain many practical ideas, exercises, activities, and other materials that can be used in faculty workshops and seminars. Course design, instructional diagnosis and improvement, goal and value clarification, faculty motivation, life and career planning, and interpersonal skills are topics dealt with.

Biggs, D., Brodie, J., and Barnhart, W. "The Dynamics of Undergraduate Academic Advising." *Research in Higher Education*, December, 1975, pp. 345-57.

> Reports a University of Minnesota study of the activities and attitudes of 452 faculty and staff academic advisors in five colleges. The four primary job activities defined were: helping students with academic, social, and financial problems; dealing with emotional concerns; providing academic and career guidance; and engaging in administrative activities. In general, advisors spent much time with academic and career guidance, less with psychological and social concerns, still less on changing values or lifestyles of advisees, and a minimum of time on study skills, financial aid or extracurricular activities information, or interpreting standardized tests for students. While most advisors were generally satisfied, one area of dissatisfaction was the lack of recognition for the work they performed.

Bligh, D. *Teaching Students*. Devon, England: Exeter University Teaching Services, 1975.

> Reviews research on seven major areas to consider when planning a course: objectives, student assessment, selecting students, course sequencing, teaching methods, analytical models of course design, and the diagnosis and treatment of course defects.

Brown, J. and Thornton, J., Jr., *College Training: A Systematic Approach*. (2d ed.) New York: McGraw-Hill, 1971.

> This useful book contains chapters on "College Students and College Teaching," "The College Professor," "A Systematic Approach to College Teaching," "Teaching and Learning Modes," "Instructional Services and Resources," and "Evaluating Instruction."

Centra, J. *Strategies for Improving College Teaching*. Washington, D.C.: American Association for Higher Education, 1972.

> A terse review of research findings on teaching and learning. Discusses self-analysis, student evaluations, and insitutional programs as ways to improve teaching. The impact of technology on teaching is also mentioned.

Christie, T. and Williamson, J. "The Counsellor—An Affective Educator." *Canadian Counsellor* 7, October, 1973, pp. 241-48.

Recommends collaboration of counselors and teachers in a program for student development. Suggests strategies counselors may use to improve classroom environment and concludes with a program which exemplifies these tactics, illustrating the contributions counselors can make to the educational process through their knowledge of human dynamics, learning processes, and motivation, and their understanding of the impact of social and environmental factors. This knowledge, combined with the academic training of teachers, can create a healthy, relevant educational setting.

Dameron, J. and Wolf, J. "Academic Advisement in Higher Education: A New Model." *Journal of College Student Personnel* 15, November, 1974, pp. 470-73.

Considers one aspect of counseling services—academic advisement—and develops a new model for incorporating this service into the overall student services program. The model for academic advisement emphasizes the student as a developing person.

Davis, J. *Teaching Strategies for the College Classroom.* Boulder, Colo.: Westview Press, 1976.

Delineates four teaching strategies and their bases in learning theory and research. The strategies include: (1) employing instructional systems based on behavior learning theory; (2) communication through lectures based on cognitive theory; (3) facilitating inquiry based on theories of thinking and reasoning; and (4) utilizing group processes based on small- and large-group theory.

Dubin, R. and Taveggia, T. *The Teaching-Learning Paradox: A Comparative Analysis of College Teaching Methods.* Eugene, Ore.: Center for Advanced Study of Education Administration, University of Oregon 97403, 1968.

This article reexamines 306 previous studies of college teaching that compared independent study, lecture instruction, discussion instruction, and variations of the three. The authors conclude that there are no differences in learning associated with the different methods of teaching.

Eble, K. *The Craft of Teaching: A Guide to Mastering the Professor's Art.* San Francisco: Jossey-Bass, 1976.

This book addresses teachers' assumptions, attitudes, and skill develoment. Modes of instruction, both within the classroom and outside, are focused upon. Practical problems in day-to-day teaching are dealt with, and improved ways to prepare teachers while in graduate school are suggested. The author believes teaching can and should be enjoyable, and that teaching skills can be learned.

Eckert, R. "New Tasks for Teachers: The Changing Personnel." *New Directions for Higher Education* 1, Winter, 1973, pp. 41-58.

Looks at four primary functions of the teacher—dreamer, designer, developer, diagnostician—with suggestions for constructive change.

Ericksen, S. *Motivation for Learning: A Guide for the Teacher of the Young Adult.* Ann Arbor, Mich.: University of Michigan Press, 1974.

Places the student at the center of the teaching process and provides a way to conceive teaching from the perspective of the learner. Transforms the findings and principles from research and theory on motivation, learning, thinking, social psychology, and personality development into practical teaching procedures. Based on several issues of the *Memo to the Faculty* newsletter, written by the author.

"Faculty Involvement in Career and Academic Advisement." *Issues in Higher Education* 10. Atlanta: Southern Regional Education Board, 1977.

Urges an effective advising system that coordinates the relationships of career to academic education and guarantees faculty contact as the way to resolve the problem of integrating a liberal arts education with career education.

Field, T. and Hecker, B. "Decentralized Community College Counselling: A Reassessment." *College Student Journal* 8, February/March, 1974, pp. 58-62.

Asserts that the purpose of counselling is to advise and place students academically. Proposes a decentralized approach to counselling characterized by an emphasis on academic specialization. Also probes the rationale for this program. Stresses the importance of eliminating barriers between counsellors and faculty, and the value of paraprofessionals in counselling.

Fiella, J. "Methods of Teaching: Ways of Turning Non-Learners into Learners." *New Frontiers in Education* 5, November, 1975, pp. 1-22.

Nine teaching methods are described and discussed with reference to types of material, learners, and teachers to which each is best suited: conditioning, habit formation, lecture, audiovisual aids, seminars, case studies, simulation games, and affective learning.

Gaff, S., Festa, C., and Gaff, J. *Professional Development: A Guide to Resources.* Change Magazine Press, 1978.

Presents several generalizations regarding teaching in higher education drawn from research, e.g., there exists no single teaching style which is best for all students or for all objectives. Provides annotated bibliographies with basic works indicated as well as lengthy general bibliographies for teaching (Faculty Development, Faculty and Teaching) and methods (Course Development). Provides a brief introduction to the literature on advising.

Gaff, J. *Toward Faculty Renewal.* San Francisco: Jossey-Bass, 1975.

Establishes a framework for instructional improvement including faculty development, instructional development, and organizational development. Describes the foci, purposes, and intellectual bases of each and gives examples of activities and programs.

Glaser, R. "Ten Untenable Assumptions of College Instruction." *Educational Record* 49, 1968, pp. 154-59.

Author identifies ten common assumptions and refutes them on the basis of his experience and research on student learning. Argues that teachers should pay greater attention to diversity of learning styles, individuality of students, and varying speed with which learning occurs. Stresses the need to organize instruction around the learning pattern of students in lieu of traditional approaches.

Groves, C. and Kennedy, E. Jr., *Career Counselor-Technician: A Progress Report.* Atlanta: Southern Regional Education Board, March, 1974.

Discusses development of a career counselor-technician program. The technician is involved in curriculum planning—incorporating faculty and student characteristics and capabilities—and advising students on both curricular and occupational matters.

Hardee, M. *Faculty Advising in Colleges and Universities.* Student Personnel Series No. 9. Washington, D.C.: American Personnel and Guidance Association, 1970.

States the problem of coordinating faculty advisement within current learning environments. Suggests roles of advisors and discusses organizational practices, stereotypes of faculty advisement, advisor preparation, and program evaluation, with good institutional examples. Advocates funded, well-planned efforts that involve inservice training, administrative support, and coordination with all student services.

Jamison, D., Suppes, P., and Wells, S. "The Effectiveness of Alternative Instructional Media: A Survey." *Review of Educational Research* 44 (1), 1974, pp. 1-67.

Review of literature on traditional methods, use of radio, television, programmed instruction and computer-assisted instruction.

Kopplin, D. and Rice, L. "Consulting With Faculty: Necessary and Possible." *Personnel and Guidance Journal* 53, January, 1975, pp. 367-72.

Explains how counselors can work more effectively by consulting with professors, either individually or in a program of consultation with the entire faculty. Establishes that the primary "care-givers" for students with problems are the teaching staff and peer counselors; therefore, training and cooperating with faculty will result in more effective advising.

Kramer, H. and Gardner, R. *Advising by Faculty.* Washington, D.C.: National Education Association, 1977.

Describes little-discussed aspects of faculty advising including roles, methodologies, relationships, special problems, and models for advising. Also delineates the concept and practice of an advising contract. Written so that reader becomes actively involved in the analysis of advising.

Kurlander, E. "Attitudes Toward College—A Counseling Priority." *New York State Personnel and Guidance Journal* 9(1), pp. 33-36.

Urges counselors to confront students with the fact that a college degree no longer guarantees economic success, discusses three divergent views of goals of liberal educators, and advises counselors to help students come to grips with their personal motivation in attending college.

Lindquist, J., ed. *Designing Teaching Improvement Programs*. Washington, D.C.: Council for the Advancement of Small Colleges, 1978.

Chapters on purposes, structure, staffing, activities, funding, and evaluation of teaching improvement programs in five different settings: liberal arts colleges (William Bergquist), universities (Claude Mathis), community colleges (Chester Chase), nontraditional institutions (Thomas Clark), and interinstitutional programs (Lance Buhl). Strategies for implementing programs are detailed.

McKeachie, W. *Teaching Tips: A Guidebook for the Beginning College Teacher*. 6th ed., Lexington, Mass.: D.C. Heath, 1969.

Offers numerous effective teaching strategies and general advice on testing of methods. Widely quoted, an idealistic yet practical guidebook for a beginning college teacher. Preparing for a course, meeting a class for the first time, lecturing, organizing effective discussion, grading, the psychology of learning, student ratings of faculty—all are colorfully reviewed, tempered by personal experience.

McKeachie, W. and Kulik, J. "Effective College Teaching." In F. Kerlinger, ed. *Review of Research in Education*. Itasca, Ill.: F. E. Peacock, 1975.

A thorough summary of the extensive research on various teaching approaches. Includes discussion of individualized instruction; educational technology (television, programmed learning, computer-assisted instruction, simulation and games); methods emphasizing student interaction and autonomy (class size, students as teachers, discussion, independent study, learning constracts); characteristics of students affecting teaching effectiveness; and structure, content, and information-processing strategies. Extensive bibliography of the research literature.

Millar, J. "Two Aspects of the Teaching-Learning Process." *Improving College and University Teaching* 22, Spring, 1974, pp. 117-19.

Cites teaching as a tool to establish new reference points, transcending the student's experiences. This is necessary to bridge the gap between what student and teacher define as relevant. Includes discussion and analysis of organization and feedback to improve instructional procedures.

Milton, O., ed. *On College Teaching*. San Francisco: Jossey-Bass, 1978.

Collection of essays covering general instructional practices such as writing objectives, testing, lecturing, and leading discussions, as well as descriptions of several approaches designed to increase student involvement, comments on "older students," a review of research on the evaluation of teaching, and suggestions for further reading.

Milton, O. *Alternatives to the Traditional: How Professors Teach and How Students Learn*. San Francisco: Jossey-Bass, 1972.

Traditional instructional practices demand reappraisal, yet a strange emotional aura keeps faculty, students, and the public from looking clearly at learning and teaching. The author provides a practical, factual basis for making decisions: research evidence about how college students learn.

Morgan, R. "A New Dimension in Community College Education: John Dewey Revisited." *Community College Social Science Journal* 1 (2), pp. 74-77.

Recommends integrating vocational instruction with liberal arts education, career exploration studies, and career group counseling.

*National Association of Student Personnel Administrators Journal* 14, Winter, 1977.

The entire issue deals with several aspects of faculty advising. Includes discussions of faculty perceptions of advising, training faculty in helping skills, student development educators as faculty developers, and a management system for faculty advising.

Ognibene, R. "The Art of Teaching: A Critical Re-Examination." *Improving College and University Teaching* 23, Summer, 1975, pp. 190-92.

The author argues that historical views of teaching as articulated here by Highet assume that students are able and motivated to learn from knowledgeable teachers. But with the increase in numbers of students lacking academic skills or motivation, teachers need to be far more sophisticated in understanding students, motivating them, and helping them to learn. Improvement in teaching involves far more than mastery of subject matter and elegant presentations.

Rogers, C. *Freedom to Learn.* Columbus, Ohio: Merrill, 1969.
A discussion of teaching and learning by a psychotherapist who emphasizes the importance of interpersonal relationships in education. Contains philosophical perspectives as well as practical ways to enhance the personal growth of both students and faculty.

Scholl, S. and Inglis, S., eds. *Teaching in Higher Education: Readings for Faculty.* Columbus: Ohio Board of Regents, 1977. Ohio Wesleyan University Bookstore, Delaware, Ohio 43015.
Contains a sampling of over three dozen exceptionally helpful papers on teaching. Articles are arranged under theory and design of instruction, alternate modes of instruction, testing and grading, evaluation of teaching, and faculty development.

Sheffield, E., ed. *Teaching in the Universities: No One Way.* Montreal/London: McGill-Queens University Press, 1974.
Twenty-four professors and a thousand graduates identify the elements of good teaching. A fine overview which illuminates certain flaws in university teaching: that professors have faulty conceptions of what teaching is, should be, and could be, and that professors may be self-deceived about student outcomes.

Stein, G. and Spille, H. "Academic Advising Reaches Out." *Personnel and Guidance Journal* 53, September, 1974, pp. 61-64.
Outlines a plan in which the counseling staff goes out on the campus to reach students in a variety of ways. The program has doubled the number of office appointments, decreased student procrastination through reminders of important deadlines, and increased informal interaction between students and advisors. Plans for the future include a cross-indexed timetable of information and academic regulations, a question-answer bulletin board, and a planning advisory group of students, advisors, and bureaucratic personnel capable of supplying immediate feedback on administrative decisions and procedures.

Travers, R., ed. *Second Handbook of Research on Teaching.* Chicago: Rand McNally, 1973.
This compendium of theory and research covers virtually all aspects of teaching. A valuable resource work.

## ADDITIONAL BIBLIOGRAPHY

Abel, E. "Liberal Learning: A Tradition with a Future." *Liberal Education,* May, 1978, 115-121.

Aitken, C. and Conrad, C. "Improving Academic Advising through Computerization." *College and University,* Fall, 1977, pp. 115-23.

Association for Supervision and Curriculum Development. "Educational Leadership: Learning Styles." *Journal of the Association for Supervision and Curriculum Development,* January, 1979.

Austenson, R. "History and the Humanities: An Integrative Approach." *Social Studies* 66, No. 5, Sept./Oct., 1975, pp. 210-14.

Austin College, Sherman, Texas. "Changing Tasks and Roles in Higher Education: A Total Institutional Project at Austin College." *Research in Education.* ERIC ED 125 488.

Averill, L. "1964: Viability of Liberal Arts." In G. Smith, ed., *Twenty-Five Years: 1945 to 1970.* San Francisco: Jossey-Bass, 1970, 160-170.

Banathy, B. *Instructional Systems.* Belmont, Calif.: Fearon, 1968.

Barnes, T. "Theory, Methodology, and Content in American Studies: A Design for a Model Course for General Education Students." *Community College Social Science Quarterly,* February, 1975, pp. 83-90.

Bess, J. "Integrating Faculty and Student Life Cycles." *Review of Educational Research,* Fall, 1973, pp. 377-403.

Bess, J. "The Motivation to Teach." *Journal of Higher Education,* May/June, 1977, pp. 243-58.

Blai, B., Jr. "Effective College Teaching Facilitates Student Thinking." *College Student Journal,* February/March, 1975, pp. 72-74.

Bossenmaier, M. "Faculty Perceptions of Academic Advising." *Nursing Outlook,* March, 1978, pp. 191-4.

Boylan, H. "Problems and Potentials of Individualized Instruction for Disadvantaged Students." Paper presented at the Eighth Annual Conference of the International Congress for Individualized Instruction. Boston, Mass., November 19, 1976. *Research in Education,* November, 1977, ERIC ED 140 864.

Buxton, T. and Keith, W. *Excellence in University Teaching.* Columbia, S.C.: University of South Carolina Press, 1975.

Centra, J., ed. "Renewing and Evaluating Teaching." *New Directions in Higher Education* 17. San Francisco: Jossey-Bass, 1977.

Coleman, J. "Differences Between Experimental and Classroom Learning." In M. Keeton and Associates, *Experimental Learning: Rationale, Characteristics, and Assessment.* San Francisco: Jossey-Bass, 1976.

Cross, P. *Beyond the Open Door.* San Francisco: Jossey-Bass, 1971.

Cross, P. "Not *Can,* But *Will* College Teaching Be Improved?" *New Directions For Higher Education* 17, San Francisco: Jossey-Bass, Spring, 1977, pp. 1-16.

Davis, R. "Learning by Design." *New Directions for Higher Education* 17, San Francisco: Jossey-Bass, Spring, 1977, 17-32.

Dearing, B. "Abuses in Undergraduate Teaching: 1965." In G. Smith, ed., *Twenty-Five Years: 1945 to 1970.* San Francisco: Jossey-Bass, 1970.

Dressel, P. *Handbook of Academic Evaluation.* San Francisco: Jossey-Bass, 1976.

Dressel, P. and Thompson, M. *Independent Study: A New Interpretation of Concepts, Practices, and Problems.* San Francisco: Jossey-Bass, 1970.

Eble, K. *Professors as Teachers.* San Francisco: Jossey-Bass, 1972.

"Educational Leadership: Learning Styles." *Journal of the Association for Supervision and Curriculum Development,* January, 1979.

Feldman, R. "Approaching English Composition as a Peer-Group Learning Experience: A Case Study." *Alternative Higher Education,* Vol. 2, 1978, pp. 237-44.

Florek, T. "Freshman Studies Program: A Handbook for Teachers." *Research in Education,* August, pp. 19-17. ERIC ED 136 704.

Fredo, D., et al. "Should Students Be Advised against Majoring in Areas of Study Where Job Prospects are Weak?" *Change,* June/July, 1978, pp. 66-68.

Gaff, J., ed. "Institutional Renewal through the Improvement of Teaching." *New Directions in Higher Education* 24. San Francisco: Jossey-Bass, 1978.

Gaff, J. and Wilson, R. "The Teaching Environment." *AAUP Bulletin,* 1971, pp. 475-93.

Garfield, L. and McHugh, E. "Learning Counseling." *Journal of Higher Education,* July/August, 1978, pp. 382-92.

Goldsmith, C. "Disciplines: Resources for Faculty Development with Sociologists." *POD Quarterly,* 1, No. 1, Spring, 1979, pp. 59-60.

Grant, G. *On Competence.* San Francisco: Jossey-Bass, 1971.

Greeley, W., et al. Report on the Visit to the Evergreen State College, Olympia, Washington. May, 1974, Unified-Studies Report No. 1:1. Boston State College, Massachusetts. *Research in Education,* ERIC ED 118 035.

Green, S. "A General Departmental Outline for Career Guidance and a Specific Outline for a Basic Career Planning Course at Pasadena City College." *Research in Education,* February, 1976, ERIC ED 112 978.

Group for Human Development in Higher Education. *Faculty Development in a Time of Retrenchment.* New Rochelle, New York: Change Magazine Press, 1974.

Hadley, E. "Helping Faculty Advisors Deal With Vocational Indecision." *Vocational Guidance Quarterly* 23, March, 1975, pp. 232-35.

Highet, G. *The Art of Teaching.* New York: Knopf, 1950.

Janaro, R. "Micronizing the Humanities: A Communal Approach." *New Directions for Community Colleges,* Winter, 1975, p. 77.

Katz, J., ed. "Services to Students." *New Directions in Higher Education* 3. San Francisco: Jossey-Bass, Autumn, 1973.

Kelly, S. "Effective College Teaching Techniques." *Improving College and University Teaching,* Spring, 1975, pp. 69-70.

Knapp, R. "Changing Functions of the College Professor." In N. Sanford, ed., *The American College: A Psychological and Social Interpretation of the Higher Learning.* New York: John Wiley, 1962.

Kozma, R. "Learning and the Instructional System." *New Directions for Higher Education* 17, Spring, 1977. San Francisco: Jossey-Bass, pp. 33-48.

Kozma, R., Belle, L., and Williams, G. *Instructional Techniques in Higher Education.* Englewood Cliffs, New Jersey: Educational Technology Publications, 1978.

Lee, C., ed. *Improving College Teaching.* Washington, D.C.: American Council on Education, 1967.

Levine, A. and Weingart, J. *Reform of Undergraduate Education*. San Francisco: Jossey-Bass, 1973.

MacDonald, G. *Five Experimental Colleges*. New York: Harper and Row, 1972.

MacMillan, T. "The Change Project at Mendocino College: Achieving Consensus on Curriculum Goals for an Integrated Liberal Arts Curriculum." Paper presented at the annual meeting of the American Association of Community and Junior Colleges (Seattle, Washington, April 13-16, 1975) *Research in Education*, ERIC ED 113 003.

Mahoney, J., Bogard, J., and Hornbuckle, P. "The Relationship of Faculty Experience and Advisee Load to Perceptions of Academic Advising." *Journal of College Student Personnel*, January, 1978, pp. 28-32.

Mash, D. "Academic Advising: Too Often Taken for Granted." *College Board Review*. Spring, 1978, pp. 33-36.

Mayhew, L. and Ford, P. *Changing the Curriculum*. San Francisco: Jossey-Bass, 1971.

Mayhew, L. *Colleges Today and Tomorrow*. San Francisco: Jossey-Bass, 1969.

Morstain, B. and Gaff, J. "Student Views of Teaching Improvement." *Educational Record*, Summer, 1977, pp. 298-308.

Nash, P. "Gentrain: An Instructional Delivery System." *New Directions for Community Colleges*. San Francisco: Jossey-Bass, Winter, 1975, 49-56.

O'Brien, C., Johnson, J., and Miller, B. "Counseling the Aging: Some Practical Considerations." *Personnel and Guidance Journal*, February, 1979, pp. 288-91.

Owens, L. "Analogs of Teaching." *Improving College and University Teaching*, Winter, 1978, pp. 11-16.

Parker, C., Good, L., and Vermillion, W., Jr. "Perceived Value of Advisors' Characteristics." *Perceptual and Motor Skills*, October, 1976, p. 678.

Perry, W. "Studying and the Student." *Higher Education Bulletin*, Summer, 1977, pp. 119-57.

Phenix, P. "Teaching as Celebration." In T. Buxton and K. Prichard, eds., *Excellence in University Teaching*, Columbia, S.C.: University of South Carolina Press, 1975, pp. 22-29.

*PIRIT Newsletter*. Project on Institutional Renewal through the Improvement of Teaching, 1818 R. Street, N.W., Washington, D.C. 20009.

Rainsford, G. "Education for the Future." *Liberal Education*, March, 1978, pp. 3-11.

Rayfield, G., Roberts, A., and Trombley, T. *National Conference on Academic Advising: A Publication of Proceedings*. University of Vt., 337 Waterman Building, Burlington, Vermont 05405, 1978.

Redditt, P. and Hamilton, W. "Teaching Improvement in a Small College." *Institutional Renewal Through the Improvement of Teaching*. In J. Gaff, ed., *New Directions for Higher Education*, 24, pp. 36-38.

Rosen, S. and Revak, R. "Science for the Non-Scientist: A Creative Effort." *Science Education*, October, 1972, pp. 513-18.

Sheffield, W. and Meskill, U. "Faculty Advisor and Academic Counselor: A Pragmatic Marriage." *Journal of College Student Personnel*, 1972, pp. 28-30.

Sherman, B. and Blackburn, R. "Personal Characteristics and Teaching Effectiveness of College Faculty." *Journal of Educational Psychology*, February, 1975, pp. 124-31.

Shucard, A. "The Contributions of Faculty Development to Humanistic Teaching." *Liberal Education*, December, 1977, pp. 559-69.

Smith, D. "The Role of Special Courses and Special Teachers." *Improving College and University Teaching*, Summer, 1977, pp. 143-53, ERIC EJ 175 915.

Smith, G., ed. *Twenty-Five Years: 1945 to 1970*. Washington, D.C.: American Association for Higher Education, 1970.

Spielberg, N. and Christensen, S. " 'Seven Ideas' and 'Entertainment and the Arts': Two Courses for the Non-Science Major." *American Journal of Physics*, May, 1977.

Toft, R. "College IV: Individualized Instruction for an Entire College." Grand Valley State Colleges, Allendale, Mich., College IV. Paper presented at the Research and Technology in College and University Teaching National Conference (Atlanta, Ga., November, 1974) *Research in Education*, ERIC ED 100 362.

Voegel, G., ed. "Using Instructional Technology." *New Directions for Community Colleges* 9. San Francisco: Jossey-Bass, 1975.

Walsh, E. "Revitalizing Academic Advisement." *Personnel and Guidance Journal*, May, 1979, pp. 446-49.

White, R., et al. "Facilitating Advising through a Computerized Checklist." *College and University*, Winter, 1978, pp. 164-71.

Wilson, F., Lopis, J., and Radke, M., Jr. *The Individual and the School.* Columbus, Ohio: Collegiate Publishing Company, 1978.

Wilson, R., et al. *College Professors and Their Impact on Students.* New York: John Wiley, 1975.

Zander, A. "The Discussion Period in a College Classroom." *Memo to the Faculty.* Center for Research on Learning and Teaching, University of Michigan, Ann Arbor, Mich. 48104, March, 1979.

## PROGRAMS FOR TEACHING AND ADVISING

American College Testing Program
Seminar on Academic Advising
Iowa City, Iowa 52242
Lee Noel, Director

A series of two-day seminars and training programs are held in various parts of the country for faculty members and administrators. The emphasis is on learning the concepts, perspectives, and skills useful in developing and operating institution-wide advising programs. A related series on seminars is on reducing student attrition, one goal of effective advising.

Carnegie-Mellon University
Pittsburgh, Pennsylvania 15213
Preston Covey, Jr., Philosophy Department

A local project is developing a text, modular instructional materials, computer-assisted programs, a course and a conference on "logical and liberal learning"—essentially how to teach and learn philosophical reasoning.

East Central College Consortium
1972 Clark Avenue
Alliance, Ohio 44601
David Ragosin, Executive Director

The Consortium is conducting a project to enable faculty from member institutions to strengthen their effectiveness in teaching part-time adult students. Consortium-wide and local workshops bring together professors from common disciplines to learn alternative teaching and advising methods.

Harvey Mudd College
Claremont, California 91711
Alvin White, Professor of Mathematics

A program of seminars is conducted along with informal contacts by which professors learn to integrate issues in the humanities and the sciences. Well over 100 faculty members in the Claremont Colleges have participated in this grass-roots, activity on faculty development—"Interdisciplinary Holistic Teaching/Learning."

Ithaca College
Ithaca, New York 14850
Eloise Blanpies, Office of the Provost

Ithaca offers "developmental sections" of existing liberal arts courses in which the skills of communication and critical thinking are integrated into the regular disciplinary content. Faculty receive assistance in learning how to combine disciplinary and subcollege level teaching.

Metropolitan State University
St. Paul, Minnesota 55101
Reatha C. King, President

This institution is charged with providing non-traditional education to a largely adult population in the Twin Cities region. A student's entire curriculum is organized around the advising relationship, as an individualized curriculum is fashioned by students and their advisors.

Michigan State University
East Lansing, Michigan 48823
Educational Development Program
Robert H. Davis, Director

Since 1962 the Education Development Program has provided a range of services to faculty throughout this large, comprehensive university. Instructional improvement grants, individual consultation with faculty, instructional media production, and evaluation services are components of this effort. Several reports and written materials are available.

Murray State University
Teaching and Media Resource Center
Murray, Kentucky 42071
Luann Wilkerson, Director

Murray State has approved a new general education program. Included is a requirement that each department that offers a core course prepare a syllabus and submit it for review and approval to the Undergraduate Studies Committee. Also, new interdisciplinary courses have been specified. The Center is assisting faculty to prepare syllabi and to design and evaluate courses that are a part of this effort.

National Academic Advising Association (NACADA)
Memphis State University
Scates Hall 107D
Memphis, Tennessee 38152
Frank M. Dyer, Jr., Treasurer

As its title indicates this new organization is concerned with improving the quality of academic advising in colleges and universities. Its major activity is an annual national conference, but other functions may develop.

National Center for Educational Brokering
1211 Connecticut Ave., Suite 400
Washington, D.C. 20036
Francis L. Macy, Director

As increasing numbers of adults express needs for better information and guidance to help them make educational and career decisions; advisory services are being developed to "broker" would-be learners and learning resources. The Center aims to increase the number, quality, and support of these brokering services by providing information about adult advisement, assessment, and advocacy; by offering technical assistance to brokering organizations; and by assisting with the development of public policy in this area.

National Council for Staff, Program and Organizational Development
c/o Staff and Program Development Office
Florida Junior College at Jacksonville
21 West Church Street
Jacksonville, Florida 32202
Roland Terrell, President

This affiliation of various kinds of "developers" in community colleges holds a national conference annually. Its network draws together many individuals who are experienced in improving the quality of teaching and learning through workshops, seminars, instructional improvement grants, and other mechanisms.

Professional and Organizational Development Network in Higher Education
c/o Projects for Educational Development
1836 Euclid Avenue
Cleveland, Ohio 441151
Lance C. Buhl, Executive Director

The POD Network is an affiliation of individuals specializing in development of various kinds: faculty, instructional, administrative, organizational, or professional. It sponsors an annual meeting on trends, model programs, and activities in this emerging field and holds training workshops for persons providing these services in colleges and universities.

Stanford University
Center for Teaching and Learning
Stanford, California 94305
Michele Fisher, Director

From 1975-1978 under Danforth Foundation funding, the Center sponsored conferences and workshops on a wide range of intellectual topics for Bay Area colleges and universities. Emphasizing both substantive and pedagogical issues, these activities have frequently stressed an interdisciplinary approach. Useful advice regarding integrative learning is available from the Center. Since 1978, the Center has been a Stanford University office organizing teaching improvement programs for teaching assistants and faculty on campus.

Syracuse University
Center for Instructional Development
Syracuse, New York 13210
Robert M. Diamond, Assistant Vice Chancellor

The Center has worked with many faculty members and departments in designing courses and curricula. When Syracuse adopted a new general education program recently, the Center helped teams of faculty develop courses appropriate to the new curriculum, particularly those dealing with interdisciplinary or thematic topics and with basic skills. It is actively involved in the design and implementation of the evaluation of the overall program and the elements within it.

University of Michigan
Center for Research on Learning and Teaching
Ann Arbor, Michigan 48104
Wilbert J. McKeachie, Director

The Center conducts research on several topics related to learning and teaching, holds workshops and seminars for faculty, works with teaching assistants, provides individual consultation, and publishes a cogent and readable newsletter entitled *Memo to the Faculty*. The large staff is knowledgeable about many aspects of instruction.

University of Tennessee
Seminar on Teaching for Graduate Teaching Assistants
Knoxville, Tennessee 37916
Russell French, Professor of Curriculum Instruction

Under the direction of the Faculty Senate Committee on Instructional Improvement, a three-credit graduate course of graduate teaching assistants has been developed. The course focuses on techniques of developing teaching skills, such as writing clear course objectives, test construction, leading discussion seminars, etc. All students in the course are required to video tape a teaching session, observe other teaching situations, and maintain a reflective journal on their reactions to readings and class presentations. The course is team taught by faculty from three different colleges.

Virginia Commonwealth University
Center for Improving Teaching Effectiveness
Richmond, Virginia 23284
John F. Noonan, Director

This teaching improvement program has accumulated a great deal of experience in ways of improving teaching and enhancing the work of faculty groups. Teaching styles, clarification of assumptions about teaching and learning, faculty evaluations, and similar topics have been pursued in depth.

# 8. Initiating and Implementing Institutional Change

## by Clifton F. Conrad

While President of Princeton University, Woodrow Wilson once complained that "reforming a college curriculum is as difficult as moving a graveyard." Nowhere is the purported rigidity of the college curriculum more striking than in the area of general education. Yet as previous chapters of this volume make abundantly clear, colleges and universities do make changes in general education. Indeed, history indicates that there are periods when large numbers of institutions reexamine their curricular commitment to liberal education, often introducing major changes in general education. We now seem to be in the midst of such a period of reexamination.

Despite numerous experiments in general education during this century, only a handful of scholars have studied academic change prior to this decade. In recent years a sizable body of research has developed on organizational change in general, as well as academic change in particular; in addition, a few researchers have begun to concentrate more specifically on the study of change in the general education component of the curriculum. However, since there is only a limited body of research specifically related to general education, this chapter will freely draw upon the organizational and general academic change literature, much of which can be applied to general education reform.

The process of change can be divided into two major stages, intiation and implementation. The initiation stage includes all those pressures and procedures leading up to, and including, the decision to introduce an innovation. And, as the term suggests, the implementation stage refers to the process of carrying out and institutionalizing the change. Since both stages are necessary for the reform of a general education program, each will be discussed.

## ALTERNATIVE MODELS OF ACADEMIC CHANGE

From the growing body of literature on institutional change, several models have emerged to guide investigative efforts. Most studies of change can be categorized within either the planned change approach or the political approach. The key different between theorists adopting the two major approaches to academic change lies in the manner in which an organization responds to various pressures which typically come from outside the institution. The two models are described briefly below.

Bennis, Benne, and Chin (1962, p. 3) define planned changes as a "conscious, deliberate, and collaborative effort to improve the operation of a system through the utilization of scientific knowledge." Basically, the planned change perspective suggests that changes within an organization can be rational and intentional. Planned change theorists assume that leaders within an institution can control the rate and direction of change through the application of knowledge gained from the behavioral sciences and/or employment of a change agent (Bennis, Benne, and Chin, 1962; Havelock, 1971 and 1972; Zaltman, Duncan, and Holbek, 1973). Lindquist's writing, particularly his *Strategies for Change* (1978), expands upon Havelock's research and represents some of the most recent work in the area. After examining and testing existing theories of change by studying case histories of colleges and universities attempting to bring about reform, Lindquist postulates a theory of change which describes innovation in terms of "adaptive development." The five keys to successful change in each stage of the adaptive development model are "interpersonal and informational linkage, active openness, facilitating as well as initiating leadership, ownership by those who can make implementation happen, and rewards both material and psychic" (Lindquist, 1978, p. 243). His major conclusion is that planned change requires the integration of several strategies, the combination of several roles and skills, and the establishment of various services designed to facilitate adaptive development.

In contrast to the planned change approach, a political perspective focuses on organizational problems and processes which are difficult to control. According to a political model, change and innovation are influenced primarily by the formation of interest groups and the resulting power conflicts; the informal social structure of the organization is the key element in analyzing the organization's response to pressures for change. Therefore, a political model helps to explain why an organization often seems incapable of facilitating change through a rational planning process.

The political model was developed and applied to higher education by Baldridge (1971) in his in-depth case study of decision making at New York University. According to Baldridge, the political maneuvering among vested interest groups is the key element of activating the change process. Other theorists also have applied a political perspective to organizational innovation (Conrad, 1978; Harvey and Mills, 1970). In a recent investigation of the change process, Conrad has focused on the sources, internal dynamics, and agents involved in college and university decision making. Following an investigation and analysis of the developments leading to the reform of general education at four postsecondary institutions, he developed a theory of academic change which ties together a series of primarily political concepts and processes. In brief, this theory identifies several major processes linking pressures for change and policy decisions to change: Conflict and interest group pressures followed by power exertion, administrative leadership, faculty leadership exercised through interest group advocacy, and compromises negotiated through administrative leadership (Conrad, 1978, p. 101).

For the curriculum reformer there are two major limitations in the literature on institutional change. First, there is no comprehensive theory on academic change, because existing theories fail to explain adequately both the initiation and implementation stages, especially of those reforms geared toward general education. Persons using a political model focus almost exclusively on internal political dynamics and give little attention to the implementation process; on the other hand, advocates of a planned change approach often ignore the focus and influence of political factors as they affect the decision to change, though they do give more attention to the implementation stage. Indeed, it often appears that one approach complements the other. But there are gaps of unexplained territory and more than a few discrepancies in interpreting events, causes, and processes in the collective body of material on academic change. The result has been a proliferation of empirical research but incomplete theoretical development.

Second, a gap still exists between research on innovation and actual strategies for change. This stems from several characteristics of the research: there has been a focus on factors and processes that are difficult to control; the policy implications of much of the innovation research are not extrapolated; and alternative strategies for change that follow from the research have not been adequately tested.

In spite of these limitations, the two major theoretical approaches to change and the body of empirical research do suggest a variety of practical strategies that can be employed by curriculum reformers. The following section builds upon the insights of the existing literature, incorporating elements suggested in both major approaches and drawing on the experience of those involved in academic reform.

## STRATEGIES FOR CHANGE

The history of general education is replete with thwarted attempts to reinvigorate the liberal tradition. Yet the success of a notable number of such reforms suggests strategies for the initiation and implementation of innovation in general education. Four major aspects of the change process seem to be critical: 1) creating a favorable climate for change; 2) building faculty support; 3) exerting administrative leadership; and 4) organizing for implementation.

Using these four as organizing strategies to suggest the scope of an overall change strategy, what follows are several approaches that may be useful for those involved in the process of curriculum change. Under each aspect, a number of specific strategies are recommended for consideration. These strategies reflect the experiences of many, but their ultimate usefulness depends upon how they are used and the general organizational context in which they are employed. It is quite possible that a strategy might be successful in one setting and be inappropriate in another.

## CREATE A CLIMATE FOR CHANGE

Colleges and universities are generally resistant to undergraduate innovation because of a number of distinctive characteristics: their purposes are basically conservative; their institutional reputation is seldom based on innovation; they emphasize rituals and traditions that often unwittingly serve to undermine attempts at change; and they are controlled by professional academics, many with lifetime tenure, who usually have a strong vested interest in maintaining the status quo (Hefferlin, 1969; Baldridge, 1975).

To overcome this inertia and potential opposition, a sound strategy for change begins by acknowledging that organizational culture and structure, as well as individual attitudes, tend to support the status quo. As a first step, proponents of change need to create a favorable climate; the following techniques may help.

*Create the Need for Change.* Throughout the change process, advocates must help to raise the awareness that improvement is needed. Advocates can aid in demonstrating the need for change in a variety of ways. One approach to promote change in general education might be to persuade faculty and administrators that the diverse types of new students currently being enrolled suggest that a new program of general education is long overdue. Or there may be pragmatic reasons such as the threat of financial exigency that require review. Some of the most distinctive innovations in general education, such as the Great Books program at St. John's College, were initiated because proponents of innovation effectively created and demonstrated the need for change.

*Communicate and Publicize the Proposal.* Along with creating the need for change, proponents of innovation should continually seek to communicate and publicize proposed changes. Advocates can use both formal (newsletters, committee meetings, and workshops) and informal (brown bag lunches, conversation in the faculty lounge, and visiting faculty in offices) channels of communication.

## BUILD FACULTY SUPPORT

A climate receptive to change can exist indefinitely without a concomitant demand for change. If there are no pressures, little change is likely to occur until the expressed need turns into a demand for change. In order to bring about change, advocates—be they faculty, administrators, students, or others from outside the institution—need to understand and influence the political character of the relevant decision making processes within the college. Because faculty have major responsibility for deciding upon and implementing changes in general education, building substantial faculty support for proposed reforms is an essential component of the overall strategy.

Although the impetus for change usually emanates from individual faculty members, the primary retardant of curricular change is more often than not the faculty-at-large. Faculty opposition usually can be attributed to two major factors. First, most faculty are concerned more with the issues of their discipline than with the curriculum as a whole. Second, academic departments usually dominate the college setting, making unacceptable any reforms which threaten the hegemony of the department.

In light of these factors, it is not surprising that many innovations in general education, such as core courses, team taught programs, and other nondepartmental offerings, receive little faculty support at the initiation stage. Perhaps more significantly, even if such innovations are accepted and institutionalized, faculty indifference is often responsible for their eventual failure (Levine and Weingart, 1973). In order to overcome potential resistance and actually win widespread support from the faculty, an effective strategy for change would include various approaches for building faculty support for innovation at both the initiation and implementation stages.

*Utilize Opinion Leaders to Persuade Others.* Innovation diffusion researchers have found that opinion leaders, those people to whom others turn for advice, are an essential component of the successful change process. As Hovland and Weiss (1967, p. 25) summarize, "The most consistent finding so far is that the most persuasive communicator is one whose expertise, experience, or social role establishes him as a credible source of the information presented."

In higher education, a small group of faculty and/or administrators is usually associated with an innovation in general education. In many cases, these individuals are not the major opinion leaders on the campus, and the innovation either fails to become institutionalized in the first place or dies gradually for lack of widespread faculty and administrative support. Instead of relying on a handful of supporters who may not include key opinion leaders on campus, effective change strategists need to discover who the opinion leaders are and seek to persuade them to persuade others (Lindquist, 1978).

*Involve a Wide Range of Faculty.* While opinion leaders are a crucial ingredient in building support for change, change proponents are well advised to involve a wide range of faculty in the process. By initiating and maintaining contact with all faculty through personal communication and bridge-building, the climate for change is considerably enhanced; innovators can cultivate and develop trust, commitment, and a sense of broad faculty ownership. Overlooking the need to include a broad base of support can mean not building sufficient groundwork for coalition formation and effective implementation. Often skeptics and opponents are not involved in the change process. Once an innovation is implemented, building support for it might involve asking skeptics or dissidents to review various aspects of the new program, such as observing a class, looking over course outlines and syllabi, and actually taking part as guest professors (Lindquist, 1977).

*Establish the Compatibility of the Change.* To help facilitate and build faculty support for innovation, change strategests pay particular attention to establishing the compatibility of the change with the norms, values, and traditions of the institution and the faculty. An effective, low profile strategy is to persuade others that the desired change is actually a reform—an effort to return the institution to its true goals and traditional purposes—rather than a transformation aimed at changing the fundamental purposes of the institution or deflecting it from its original aims (Martorana and Kuhns, 1975). Thus, a new core curriculum might be hailed not as a revolutionary alternative to an outmoded distribution system of general education, but as a better means of fulfilling an institution's long-standing objectives. By establishing the compatibility of the innovation, change proponents are more likely to dissuade doubters that the innovation seriously threatens the historic mission of the school, enabling proponents to retain more control over the nature and direction of the change.

*Emphasize the Benefits of the Innovation for Faculty.* Change strategists may go a step beyond establishing the compability of an innovation; they may also identify and emphasize the profitability of the change, the degree to which a change satisfies personal and/or group needs *(Levine, 1978). The more that faculty perceive an innovation as congruent with their self-interest, the greater the likelihood of faculty support for innovation and successful reform. At the organizational level, particularly at the departmental level, it is wise to demonstrate how a particular innovation will be profitable. For example, an innovation adopted at one institution, such as a new freshman seminar program, which results in increased enrollment or a large foundation grant might motivate a faculty elsewhere to adopt and support a similar innovation. At the individual level, advocates can point out how proposed activities, such as developing a new interdisciplinary course, are congruent with the growth needs of faculty.

*Build Coalitions: Know When to Fight.* By effectively using opinion leaders and involving a wide range of faculty in the change process, change advocates have laid the foundation for perhaps the most critical aspect of an effective change strategy: building coalitions in favor of the proposed changes (Baldridge, 1971; Conrad, 1978; Martorana and Kuhns, 1975). In order to overcome institutional inertia and faculty resistance, coalitions are usually essential for approving an innovation in the appropriate decision making body.

In many colleges and universities, a myth still persists that of all the components of the curriculum, programs of general education are determined more by educational considerations than by political pressures. Yet much recent research clearly indicates that power blocs are critical for the successful initiation of innovative programs. Instead of lamenting the fact that colleges are splintered into divergent and overlapping groups, reformers can actively build political bases for influencing decisions. Ironically, coalition building around alternative educational proposals actually may enhance the quality of educational decisions by bringing major issues into the open. This is in contrast to many decision making procedures which may appear collegial but in reality mask a series of political compromises that remain hidden from most faculty.

*Know When to Compromise.* In their zeal for reform, some change proponents do not know when to compromise. Particularly in the area of general education, where the perception may be that proposals for reform cannot be modified without irreparable harm, a corollary strategy may be adopted: the original proposal can ask for more changes than are expected, so that compromises may be made and the result is about what was wanted in the first place.

## EXERT ADMINISTRATIVE LEADERSHIP

If faculty support for successful innovation is essential, administrative leadership may be the sine qua non for successful academic change (Ladd, 1970; Conrad, 1978). In a well known study of academic change, Hefferlin (1969) has found that professors and department chairpersons, as well as

---

*May be found in Basic Readings, Chapter 2.

administrators, view administrators as the most important group in influencing the academic program.

Within the area of general education, administrative leadership should be taken by the appropriate academic dean. Not only can this individual create and maintain an atmosphere of receptivity to change, he can be actively involved in the change process, combining initiative with involvement and serving as a mediator between various groups.

*Combine Initiative with Involvement.* While administrators can utilize various strategies for combining initiative with involvement, this strategy implies a combination of personal initiative with the ongoing attempt to involve faculty and students in the procedure (Lindquist, 1978). Administrators can facilitate the process of change by providing channels of communication among groups, bringing a shared sense of purpose, using a keen sense of timing, and keeping things moving in an orderly fashion without appearing to force an issue. Moreover, they also serve as a separate power bloc, both in terms of initiating changes in general education and exerting influence over the process (Conrad, 1978).

*Serve as a Compromiser.* Although the goals of colleges and universities, particularly in the area of general education, are usually stated so broadly as to be acceptable to nearly everyone in an institution, the means of achieving them is a major source of conflict. Even if there is relative success in building support for innovation, interest groups which resist the proposed changes will inevitably emerge. At this juncture, when conflict between interest groups becomes visible, administrative intervention is usually crucial. Administrators play an important brokering role by helping to negotiate compromises. They can use certain myths—such as collegiality—to mold consensus and delegitimize deviants (Conrad, 1978). Through judicious attempts to bring about compromises in the direction of reform and innovation, administrators give tangible support to individuals and groups advocating change while helping to break down resistance.

## ORGANIZE FOR IMPLEMENTATION

Possibly the most important and certainly the most overlooked component of successful change is the implementation process. Because their immediate concern is to secure approval for their proposed changes, many academic innovators fail to give sufficient attention to implementation. The following strategies suggest that planning for implementation should not be deferred until the implementation stage, should include several key features, and should be modified as the plan is adopted.

*Incorporate an Explicit Implementation Plan into the Proposal.* A detailed implementation plan, built into all major proposals for changing the curriculum, is important for two reasons. First, by helping to dispel faculty fears concerning the proposed changes, it promotes the successful passage of the proposal. Second, such a plan involves a larger group of faculty in deciding how it will be implemented rather than leaving it to a smaller group of overseers. Those directly affected by the change are more likely to support it if they have a role in shaping its implementation.

*Build an Effective Structure of Rewards and Resources.* A supportive system of rewards and a reallocation of resources is an important ingredient of successful curriculum change. Yet most traditional faculty reward structures discourage active faculty involvement in general education, and many implementation plans do not include proposals for modification in the reward structure. Rewards are usually associated with departments, traditional subject matter, and discipline-related activity. Teaching a new interdisciplinary course, for example, is sometimes viewed negatively in promotion, tenure, and salary considerations because it involves faculty time that could be used for disciplinary activities. Given the traditional reward structure, it is not surprising, then, that many general education programs are plagued by involuntary staff participation, high instructor turnover, little senior faculty involvement, and negative teaching evaluation *(Levine, 1978).

There are a number of ways in which reward structures can be altered to encourage greater, more enthusiastic participation in innovative general education programs. One obvious way is to modify criteria for salary increments and promotion; instead of rewarding faculty solely for discipline-related activity, a college can place equal or more emphasis on teaching in general education. In the past, this solution has been ineffective, for departments have been reluctant to rearrange reward structures in favor of teaching. Increased pressures for accountability, in teaching and in general education programs, may make it easier now to alter reward structures. A second incentive is financial assistance, perhaps during the summer, for preparing for teaching general education courses. Other minor rewards can be used, such as provision of clerical services, travel funds, and visibility to participating faculty and to the program itself (Mayhew and Ford, 1971).

*Choose an Appropriate Mechanism for Administering the Program.* Typically, the administration of general education is decentralized or shared by a college-wide academic officer and the departments offering courses that meet general education requirements. Where general education is a fully prescribed component of the curriculum, it usually is administered by the principal academic officer of the college. In a few cases, separate administrative units supervise programs of general education. In organizing for effective implementation, an administrative mechanism that provides clear responsibility and authority is necessary. Although the choice of a specific mechanism depends on contextual factors, some experts suggest that the effective implementation of change requires a fairly high degree of centralization, including a specific line of authority. This is because strict channels of authority may reduce potential conflict and ambiguity that can impair implementation (Zaltman, Duncan, and Holbek, 1973).

The Carnegie Foundation for the Advancement of Teaching *(1977) recommends that institutions consider the centralization of budgeting, financing, and evaluation of general education programs in a separate academic unit responsible for their administration. Admittedly, initiating such a unit would be difficult on most campuses, since funds must be recaptured from departments. Moreover, it poses the old problem of general education being set apart from other departmental functions and the faculty being regarded as outcasts. Still, the advantages of centralized control over a developing program in general education can be considerable.

*Select Key People for Administering the Program.* Gross and his colleagues (1971) contend that administrators can have a critical bearing on the implementation of innovation by reducing resistance and establishing and maintaining conditions which will facilitate subordinates' efforts to adapt. Specifically, administrators can: 1) provide necessary resources; 2) secure whatever retraining is required; 3) provide the appropriate supports and rewards; 4) adjust organizational arrangements and policies to make them compatible with the innovation; and 5) commit themselves to an innovation they expect subordinates to implement (Gross, Giacquinla, and Bernstein, 1971).

In many new general education programs, especially those organized around a separate administrative unit, the selection of key faculty to provide leadership for the programs is equally important. Regardless of the particular administrative mechanism adopted to oversee the changes or the previous role or position of the individual selected to assume the major supervisory role, it is imperative that individuals are chosen who are likely to administer the program effectively.

*Incorporate a Plan for Faculty Development.* Faculty members committed to a new program of general education may find it difficult to teach successfully in one no matter how gifted they may be in the departmental classroom. Their background and training may not prepare them for broad, cooperative, and often interdisciplinary teaching. Trained to be specialists, individual faculty members may have difficulty teaching interdisciplinary, skill, or core courses; taught to view themselves as independent professionals, they may have trouble with team teaching or other collaborative activities. (See Chapter 7 for further discussion about collaborative teaching.)

To promote the transition of individuals from departmental to non-departmental teaching, it is important to include a plan for faculty development in the implementation process. One approach to faculty retraining is to initiate workshops and seminars aimed at developing skills needed in a new program. Team teaching and interdisciplinary teaching skills may be needed by general education faculty. Another strategy, targeted at increasing longterm faculty collaboration, is reshuffling of offices. Most faculties are usually grouped together by department, preserving a sense of professional isolation that can undermine integration in general education. By reducing the physical or psychological distance between faculty involved in a new core curriculum, for example, the possibilities for enhanced collaboration may increase considerably.

*Make Adjustments throughout the Implementation Process.* The most carefully conceived implementation plan is unlikely to anticipate all ramifications of a new program. Unanticipated problems inevitably arise which call for ongoing adjustment to the original innovation and its implementation plan. For example, a general education program may make assumptions about course enrollment patterns which prove erroneous when the program begins. Ideally, a sound formative and summative evaluation plan (see following chapter) will enable administrators to react quickly to problems as they arise. But no matter how effective and timely the evaluation, major modifications requiring the support of supervisory staff and faculty will arise. Chief proponents of an innovation are often unwilling to change, choosing to fight for the integrity of their ideas. While there are times when proposed modifications do seem particularly inappropriate, it is sound strategy to make adjustments that reflect actual program experience.

The history of general education is replete with examples of innovations that failed largely because they were not modified to meet changing conditions and the test of practice.

In conclusion, despite the past frustrations of Woodrow Wilson and countless others who have attempted curricular innovation, change *has* taken place. However, changes frequently have been unexpected, uncontrolled, unplanned, and often unwanted. Today, unlike the past, there are social scientific models and a growing body of empirical research from which proponents of academic change can draw to plan purposefully in a way rarely possible before. The political model with its focus on conflict, power groupings, and vested interests, suggests strategies that enable change proponents to build widespread support for change. The planned change model with its emphasis on persuasion, carefully specified goals and means to achieve them, and effective interpersonal communication, points to other strategies for change. Wise change proponents will use knowledge and understanding generated from both models, choosing and adapting strategies to the special context of their own college or university.

In the past, academics have been hesitant to discuss such strategies, perhaps regarding them as too manipulative. Certainly, it is true that ultimately the "rightness" or "wrongness" of a change comes down to the quality and integrity of the proposed program itself. Nevertheless, to ignore means of successfully bringing changes to an academic organization is fatalistic, if not fatal. The soundest, most innovative ideas and plans for change in general education have often failed out of ignorance or from unwillingness to orchestrate the dynamics of the change process. Powerful ideas for change must be embodied in effective strategies for introducing those ideas and bringing them to fruition.

## ANNOTATED BIBLIOGRAPHY

Baldridge, V. "Rules for a Machiavellian Change Agent: Transforming the Entrenched Professional Organization." In J. Baldridge and T. Deal, eds. *Managing Change in Educational Organizations*, Berkeley, Calif.: McCutchan, 1975.
  The author views college and university decision-making as dominated by entrenched professionals who are more interested in serving themselves than in serving their clients. To bring about change in this politicized decision structure, change agents must adapt "Machiavellian" techniques such as building coalitions and using committees effectively.

Conrad, C. "A Grounded Theory of Academic Change." *Sociology of Education* 51. April, 1978, pp. 101-112.
  Based upon a study of major changes in general education at four institutions, the author explicates a theory of change which is based almost entirely on political concepts and processes. The theory identifies several major processes which link pressures for change and a policy decision to change: conflict and interest group pressure, administrative intervention, faculty leadership exercised through interest group advocacy, and compromises negotiated-through administrative leadership.

Havelock, R., *A Guide to Innovation in Education.* Ann Arbor, Mich.: Institute for Social Research, 1972.
  This book is a noted guide to the *process* of innovation intended for educators at all levels and positions. Change agents, in general, will find the reference format especially helpful with the division into three segments: actual case studies of innovation, theory on the stages of planned change, and several appendices outlining supplementary resources along with an annotated bibliography on change in education. In addition to its pragmatic format and thorough referencing, this manual has a broad level of applicability brought about by its concentration on the process of change, not the content.

Havelock, R. et al.,*Planning for Innovation through the Dissemination and Utilization of Scientific Knowledge*. Ann Arbor, Mich.: Institute for Social Research, 1971.

Havelock and his associates have provided a comprehensive framework for the study of the processes of innovation, dissemination of innovation, and knowledge utilization. The authors analyze characteristics of both the individual and organizations which impede or encourage the transfer; examine different models of "dissemination and utilization"; and propose a linkage model as a synthesis. Also, factors related to successful "dissemination and utilization" are discussed. The work concludes with a review of the relevant literature in education and other fields of practice within this framework.

Hefferlin, JB, *The Dynamics of Academic Reform*. San Francisco: Jossey-Bass, 1969.

Though somewhat dated, this remains the most comprehensive empirical study of academic change. Using a stratified sample of 110 American colleges and universities, the author employs a survey research strategy based on telephone interviewing. He identifies major sources, processes, correlates, and agents of academic change.

Huber, C. "The Dynamics of Change: A Core Humanities Program." *Liberal Education,* May 1977, pp. 159-170.

This provides a descriptive account of an integrated studies program "whose origin, scope and purpose are unarguably suffused with an awareness of human frailties, and educational conviction." This author argues that "we confirmed that human realities must be taken into account not only to facilitate the process of change, but in shaping its direction as well. It is not a disinterest in teaching or in the coherence and integrity of a general education program that prevents improvement. It is essentially the lack of reward and opportunity for teamwork, the refusal to offer permanent, subtle, and tangible acknowledgements for anything but routine. This constitutes a failure to satisfy the natural human venality, pride and will to succeed present in every profession."

Ladd, R. *Change in Educational Policy*. New York: McGraw-Hill, 1970.

This report, prepared for the Carnegie Commission on Higher Education, describes and evaluates both the educational policy changes proposed in 11 institutions between 1965 and 1969 and the processes by which these proposed changes were developed and disposed of by the institutions involved. The author concludes that fundamental change in educational policy is unlikely except where a significant portion of the faculty accept the desirability of some change before the study begins or where pressures for change from outside the faculties are much in evidence.

Levine, A. (b) "The Life and Death of Innovation in Higher Education." Occasional Paper No. 2. Buffalo, N.Y.: Department of Higher Education, 479 Baldy Hall, State University of New York at Buffalo, 1978.

In attempting to discover why innovations fail, a model of the institutionalization-termination process of innovation was applied in a study of "The Colleges" at the State University of New York at Buffalo. The author concludes that failure results from an innovation's decline in profitability to and compatibility with the innovating unit.

Lieberman, J. "The Pathology of Innovation." *Liberal Education,* October, 1976, pp. 380-384.

An analysis of the obstacles to change, such as legal restraints and faculty rewards, and some strategies for surmounting them.

Lindquist, J. "Curricular Implementation." In A. Chickering, et al. *Developing the College Curriculum*. Washington, D.C.: Council for the Advancement of Small Colleges, 1977.

This section of a comprehensive handbook on curriculum planning identifies obstacles to curriculum development and identifies common flaws in traditional change strategies; discusses various approaches for assessing curriculum development needs; amplifies strategies for successful change; and concludes with suggestions for implementing and evaluating curricular reform.

Lindquist, J. *Strategies for Change*. Washington, D.C.: Council for the Advancement of Small Colleges, 1978.

The author and his colleagues in the Strategies for Change and Knowledge Utilization Project initiated an in-depth study of change processes in seven diverse colleges and universities. Based on this study, the author reviews existing theories of change and knowledge utilization, then examines and tests these theories through case histories of attempts to bring about major curricular, administrative, or instructional reform. He concludes with the postulation of a new theory of change.

Maguire, J. "Can Change Be Institutionalized? How?" *Liberal Education,* December, 1977, pp. 584-589.
  Based upon an examination of four major obstacles to change, the author discusses "necessary" conditions for the effective institutionalization of change—such as compromise and learning how to sustain a reasonably strong level of commitment.

Martorana, S. and Kuhns, E. *Managing Academic Change.* San Francisco: Jossey-Bass, 1975.
  The authors present 20 detailed case studies of widely discussed innovations—from students and curriculum to facilities and finance. Each innovation is described by a contributor who has been involved in both development and implementation of change. The contributors review the strategies and tactics they employed, the background forces involved, and the lessons they learned from firsthand experience. The authors then summarize these innovations, discuss problems and opportunities, and make recommendations for those in similar situations.

Mayhew, L. and Ford, P. *Changing the Curriculum.* San Francisco: Jossey-Bass, 1973.
  This volume brings together a survey of the issues involved in change, an analysis of current curriculum practices, a study of students, specific suggestions for curriculum innovation, and a statement of the principles for solving curriculum problems. The chapter on "Mechanisms for Change" outlines six principles for change strategists.

Rogers, E. "The Communication of Innovations in a Complex Institution." *Educational Record,* Winter, 1968, pp. 67-77.
  The author reviews research dealing with the diffusion and infusion of innovation in universities. He suggests four key elements to diffusion: 1) an innovation; 2) communicating via several channels; 3) reaching many members of a social system; and 4) adopting it over a period of time. He contends that there are certain strategies of change that might speed up the diffusion process, such as "develop and select innovations for the large university that have a clear-cut relative advantage and test their effectiveness under operational conditions before adopting them on a widespread scale."

Sprunger, B., Bergquist, W., and Quehl, G. *Handbook for College Administration.* Washington, D.C.: Council for the Advancement of Small Colleges, 1978.
  Applications of management theories and practices to college administration. Illustrations, exercises, and other helpful aids can be used to develop more effective organization and to facilitate change.

Zaltman, G., Duncan, R., and Holbek, J. *Innovations and Organizations.* New York: John Wiley, 1973.
  This is a comprehensive academic treatment of innovation in organizations. It provides an excellent overview of the research on innovations, particularly on the types of innovations, the variables and conditions affecting the process of their adoption, and the kinds of environments that are conducive to the introduction and diffusion of innovations. The authors conclude the book with a useful review of the theory of innovation in organizations and a brief review of some selected theories.

## ADDITIONAL BIBLIOGRAPHY

Argyris, C. "Theories of Action that Inhibit Individual Learning." *American Psychologist,* 31, 1976, pp. 638-54.
Baldridge, J. *Power and Conflict in the University.* New York: John Wiley, 1971.
Bennis, W., Benne, K., and Chin, R., eds. *The Planning of Change.* New York: Holt, Rinehart and Winston, 1962.
Bennis, W. *Organization Development: Its Nature, Origins and Prospects.* Reading, Mass.: Addison-Wesley, 1969.
Bergquist, W., Phillips, S., and Quehl, G. *Handbook for Faculty Development.* Washington, D.C.: Council for the Advancement of Small Colleges, Vols. I and II, 1975 and 1977.
*Changing Tasks and Roles in Higher Education: A Total Institutional Project at Austin College.* Sherman, Texas: Austin College (n.d.).
Dunham, D. "On Deaning in General Education." *University College Quarterly.* East Lansing, Mich.: University College, Michigan State University, 1976, pp. 16-27.
Gross, N., Giacquinla, J., and Bernstein, M. *Implementing Organizational Innovations.* New York: Basic Books, 1971.

Harvey, E., and Mills, R. "Patterns of Organizational Adaptation: A Political Perspective." In M. Zald, ed., *Power and Organizations*. Nashville, Tenn.: Vanderbilt University Press, 1970.

Hodgkinson, H. *Institutions in Transition*. New York: McGraw-Hill, 1971.

Hovland, C. and Weiss, W. "The Influence of Source Credibility on Communication Effectiveness." In R. Rosnow and E. Robinson, eds., *Experiments in Persuasion*. New York: Academic Press, 1967.

Jencks, C. and Riesman, D. *The Academic Revolution*. Chicago: University of Chicago Press, 1968.

Levine, A. and Weingart, J. *Reform of Undergraduate Education*. San Francisco: Jossey-Bass, 1973.

Melander, E. and Pitts, E. "Faculty and Administrative Roles in Fostering Curricular Innovation." *Journal of General Education*, Summer, 1977, pp. 113-21.

Morgan, G. and Toomajian, C. "A Course Projection and Staffing Plan to Facilitate a Curriculum Change." *Research in Higher Education*, Vol. 2, 1974, pp. 109-17.

*Renewal: Institutional Change and Professional Development at Davis and Elkins College*. Elkins, West Virginia: Davis and Elkins College, 1976.

Rodgers, E. and Shoemaker, F. *Communication of Innovations*. New York: Free Press, 1971.

Ross, R. "The Institutionalization of Academic Innovations: Two Models." *Sociology of Education*, April, 1976, pp. 146-155.

Scott, R. "Curriculum Development in the Steady State: Renewing by Regrouping." *Journal of General Education*, Fall, 1977, pp. 221-27.

Sikes, W., Schlesinger, L., and Seashore, C. *Renewing Higher Education from Within*. San Francisco: Jossey-Bass, 1974.

# PROGRAMS FOR CHANGE

American Association of State Colleges and Universities
One Dupont Circle
Washington, D.C. 20036
Resource Center for Planned Change
Marina Buhler-Miko, Director

The Center has addressed the topics of faculty development, programs for new student clientele, and program evaluation while developing a model of comprehensive institutional planning entitled A Futures Creating Paradigm. A current project is the assessment of the general outcomes of undergraduate education as a means to reform the curriculum. The guidebook describing this process, *Academic Program Evaluation Paradigm*, will be released shortly.

Association of American Colleges
1818 R Street, N.W.
Washington, D.C. 20009
Project Lodestar
Regina M.J. Kyle, Vice President for Planning and Programs

In this three year project Liberal Learning Advisory Teams will assist colleges and universities in evaluating and improving their courses, curricula, and programs in liberal education. Institutional Advisory Teams will help schools review their purposes, strengthen their planning, and renew their commitment to liberal learning.

Council for the Advancement of Small Colleges
One Dupont Circle, Suite 320
Washington, D.C. 20036
National Consulting Network
Daniel H. Pilon, Vice President

Low cost consultation to liberal arts colleges is provided in over 200 topical areas. Consultants, drawn primarily from small colleges, have become involved in various kinds of educational improvements, and both generalists and specialists are available.

Los Medanos Community College
Pittsburg, California 94565
Professional Development Program
Chester Case, Professional Development Facilitator

The distinctive Los Medanos general education program was implemented with an intensive faculty development program for persons who teach in it. The College itself has been very attentive to creating a collaborative organizational climate and governance process to support the curriculum.

Miami-Dade Community College
11380 N.W. 27 Avenue
Miami, Florida 33167
Office of Management and Organizational Development
Carol Zion, Director

The Center pioneered the application of organizational development to higher education, and continues to offer workshops, seminars, and materials for faculty members and administrators at this school. A wealth of experience with the process of change at one institution has been accumulated.

Memphis State University
Memphis, Tennessee 38152
Institute for Academic Improvement
Jack Lindquist, Director

The Institute focuses on six areas: the process of planned change, adult development and learning, individualized education, experiential learning, program evaluation, and general education. It organizes and coordinates special multi-institutional projects, holds residential workshops, provides information linking services, provides consultation, and offers doctoral study in planned change and adult learning.

National Institute for Staff and Organizational Development
c/o School of Education
University of Texas–Austin
Austin, Texas 78703
John E. Roueche, Director

The Institute concentrates its work in teaching and learning for non-traditional students, primarily in community colleges. Workshops, seminars, and materials are characteristic activities.

Northeastern Illinois University
5500 N. St. Louis Avenue
Chicago, Illinois 60625
Center for Program Development
Reynold Feldman, Dean

Northeastern encourages and supports curriculum improvement efforts, such as its participation in the Project on General Education Models, through its Center for Program Development, a Fellows Program for faculty development, and a growing association of institutional members concerned with improving the education of its diverse student body.

Projects for Educational Development
1836 Euclid Avenue
Cleveland, Ohio 44115
Lance C. Buhl, President

This organization has coordinated a multi-institution regional project in which colleges and universities engage in teaching improvement, faculty evaluation, and curricular revision efforts. Currently, it operates a program to enhance the functioning of academic departments and the professional development of department chairpersons. A strong emphasis on the renewal of institutions runs through its work.

# 9.  Evaluation: Assessment, Judgment and Decision

## by Michael L. Davis

Paul Dressel (1976, p. ix) has declared that "every educational or social program is initiated and continues or is discarded because of some form of evaluation by...individuals or groups." If evaluation is an integral part of educational programs, those who shepherd an alternative or new program of general education into being consciously ought to make some provision for its evaluation. This chapter is intended to provide a basis for determining the nature of that evaluation, specifically by introducing ideas that may be key in understanding evaluation processes, clarifying some misunderstandings and suspicions about evaluation, suggesting assessment instruments and procedures, and identifying some general education programs that can be used as models when discussing evaluation.

The emphasis is this chapter is on program evaluation. Related matters of assessing student accomplishment and evaluating faculty, although important in their own right, will not be treated here, because excellent summaries in these two areas are available. Milton and Edgerly's (1976) summary of student assessment is a fruitful starting point. More detailed or comprehensive treatments are to be found in Bess (1979), Dressel (1976, Part Two), Ebel (1972), and Milton and Associates (1978, Chapters 4 and 5). In the areas of faculty evaluation and teaching assessment, an excellent resource guide (Gaff, Festa, and Gaff, 1978) is available, and more extensive treatments are to be found in Dressel (1976, Chapter 15 and 16), Doi (1974), Genova, Madoff, Chin, and Thomas (1976), Grasha (1977), Miller (1972; 1974), and North and Scholl (1978). Because these topics have been well reviewed, they are included in this summary only as they pertain to program evaluation.

Evaluation, in some form, occurs more often than is realized. In its most general form, evaluation involves a judgment that is based on an explicit or an implicit value. Evaluation includes judgments people make about the worth of something, the decision to act on the basis of judgment. Professional evaluators also argue that evaluation is the process whereby a judgment is made. This process includes the definition of goals and objectives to be met by a program of general education, for instance, the identification of

117

the criteria or values on which to base a judgment of worth, the accumulation of sound evidence on which to base judgments, and specification of implications for policy making and group action. Evaluation may, but does not necessarily, involve highly technical matters from the fields of psychological measurement, sociological assessment, and fiscal management.

Since many people are suspicious of evaluation, discussions of the topic should be undertaken with this fact in mind. Suspicions come from several sources. First, many individuals are naturally reluctant to be judged or evaluated by others. Much of the evaluation in higher education traditionally has involved the assessment of one person by another individual or group. These assessments have been far from perfect, further undermining the credibility of evaluation. Second, the complexities of any program and the larger context in which it operates may lead to conflicting interpretations of its value, even with a careful evaluation. For example, a program of general education embodies several different goals; each goal may call for different kinds of evidence to be gathered and the evidence may be subject to different interpretations. When people naively expect evaluation to produce clear results, they lose confidence when it does not produce definitive results. Finally, evaluations sometimes plunge one into esoteric matters of fiscal accountability, psychological measurement, social policy assessment, and governmental quality assurance, topics not well understood by typical curriculum planners.

From another perspective, evaluation is a very personal activity. One assigns value to something or extracts value from it on the basis of personal assumptions about what is and is not to be valued. Even the professional evaluator admits that a personal orientation to evaluation cannot be overlooked (Anderson and Ball, 1978; Dressel, 1976; Katzenmeyer, 1979; Lessinger, 1971; Stone, 1978). This has resulted in a variety of approaches to evaluation even by the experts. Indeed there appears to be no single model for overall effective evaluation.

Three general sources are important reading as one begins to consider the evaluation of higher education programs. One of these (Katzenmeyer, 1979) is an evaluation workshop presentation given to faculty members writing grant proposals to federal agencies. While the purposes of evaluation which Katzenmeyer discusses are slightly different from those of a general education program, his summary provides a common sense introduction to program evaluation written in lay language. This volume can help to demythologize evaluation and yet to enlighten curriculum planners.

A second source is Suchman (1967), one of the classics in program evaluation. He argues that evaluation is a special type of research and shows how it differs from other forms of scholarly research. Strengths and weaknesses of different models of evaluation are discussed.

The third source (Dressel, 1976) is an excellent summary of and a personal perspective on evaluation in higher education. The preface and the first two chapters are essential reading for anyone who is interested in initiating academic change. The chapters on objectives, the learning environment, educational processes, and the curriculum are insightful descriptions of the relationship of these topics to evaluation in higher education.

# SIX PHASES OF EVALUATION

Suchman (1967) describes the evaluation process in terms of six phases or activities. These six phases include: 1) the clarification of the value base for evaluation; 2) the set of goals on which to base evaluation; 3) the articulation of the goals into objectives or criteria for measurement; 4) program planning; 5) program implementation; and 6) program evaluation. Since the results of the final phase can lead back to the first, i.e., clarifying the value base, the six phases constitute a continuous and cyclical process.

Evaluation of a value base or an underlying value has been referred to as *context evaluation.* This typically refers to the judgment that some course of action or intervention is justified because the status quo is inadequate. The data gathering activities included in context evaluation are often described as "needs assessment" and have been summarized by Scriven and Roth (1978). For example, a need may be suggested by the fact that large numbers of the incoming freshmen class are deficient in reading comprehension or expository writing ability. On the basis of presumed values, the faculty might anticipate that these students would have difficulty completing their college work. This is a presumed need to be supported with corroborating evidence before a full-scale program is planned. A needs assessment could be directed at identifying students who had previously been admitted with similarly defined deficiencies and reviewing their college records to ascertain the degree of success they had in coursework. Further, a brief questionnaire could be distributed to obtain some idea about their career patterns since leaving the college or university.

Once needs have been defined they can be restated into goals or objectives. Assuming that the needs assessment indicated that students admitted with verbal deficiencies had special difficulties completing college, the faculty could state a goal. In this case, the goal statement might read: "Students with verbal deficiencies should improve their reading and writing skills to acceptable levels."

Having set the goals, the faculty would need to agree upon the measurement of goal attainment. This might mean nothing more than readministering the original measures to these students, or it might mean developing another assessment procedure to be administered at the end of the students' freshmen or sophomore year. Assessment should be carefully considered. If possible, consulting colleagues who have expertise in psychological measurement, interviewing and statistics is well worth the effort. A very useful listing of assessment instruments is included in Bess (1979).

The program planning process is particularly crucial and difficult in higher education. This is the phase when decisions are made about the nature of a new or revised program. Evaluation during this phase is designed to assist and inform decisions about the choice among many possible programs, and it should address specific questions. First, what are the particular needs the program must satisfy? Why would any one program be expected to accomplish these needs? Which option looks best, and why? What is the anticipated cost of operating the best choice? What resources will be required to initiate the best choice option, and for how long? Some people refer to this type of evaluation as *input evaluation* or *front end analysis.* It should tell you what inputs are needed or what the up front costs are.

119

A few words of caution about input evaluation. It can be both expensive and difficult. Ideally, there would be a body of research that could guide decisions about the desirability of different options. In fact, we have very little good research about general education programs and only slightly more clear documentation about the nature of specific programs. Therefore, comparisons of model general education programs are likely to be heavily influenced by faculty attitudes, by trends in arts, sciences and humanities disciplines, and by economic factors. While these can be assessed and summarized, they are also likely to change over time. Because of this instability and because of a tradition against expensive planning efforts, it is difficult to justify the expenses associated with thorough program planning. Several effective and efficient models for program planning do exist and should be considered (Coldeway, 1979; Winstead, 1976). Some program planning and evaluation models can be gradually adopted. In addition to the political and psychological advantages of gradual adoption, the costs of a systematic planning and evaluation procedure within a particular department, college or school are sometimes more manageable if they are distributed over a long period of time.

The fifth phase in Suchman's model is the program implementation and operation phase. There are three evaluation-related activities that are essential at this phase. First, program administration and management must obtain and retain data that will be used in evaluating the program. In the above example, if the poorly qualified students are admitted, care should be taken to preserve entry level scores for possible comparison with the results that may be found from later testing. Further, records of the students' experiences in reading and writing would need to be kept; additional measures might be administered; and the data would need to be stored in a convenient form.

A second evaluation activity that should be included in program implementation is called *formative evaluation*. As one initiates any new program there are minor adjustments that should be made. Sometimes these can be made on the basis of common sense; in other cases a more considered decision may be required. Evaluators have suggested that program monitoring should be carefully planned so that information is available to support the more difficult decisions about program revisions (Grant, 1978). In this sense, formative evaluation refers to decisions that affect the form of an ongoing program. Formative evaluation can be contrasted to *summative evaluation* that summarizes the good or value associated with a particular program. Summative evaluation represents the final judgment about the strengths and weaknesses of a program.

Charters and Jones (1973) question the appropriateness of a laboratory-type research model for educational and social evaluation. In the natural setting of a college's general education program an intervention cannot be assumed to occur for all students, regardless of how carefully that intervention has been planned. Suppose that the poorly qualified students, in the above example, were admitted and enrolled into specially designed courses that were expected to accelerate their verbal learning. Assuming that the instruction had occurred, an evaluation was performed by comparing the students' average pre-course score with their average post-course score. A slight average improvement in scores was obtained, but the improvement did not come close to the average post-course score from a sample of "properly" qualified students. Should the college decide the program failed, discontinue it and no longer admit students with low verbal scores? One cannot tell. It is possible that many of the poorly qualified students greatly profited from the course. However, the average score for the poorly qualified students showed little gain because some of these students rarely attended classes and consequently obtained very low scores. For these students the class, or intervention, never occurred. The effectiveness of the intervention could not be assessed on the basis of these students' post-course scores. Therefore, programs must be monitored to determine that they are reaching the intended audience.

In summary, evaluation does occur during the program implementation and maintenance phase. Assessments and data analyses should be conducted; information should be obtained to help improve the program; and steps should be taken to assure that the program is reaching its intended audience.

The sixth phase in Suchman's model is the program evaluation phase. In many respects, the term summative evaluation is appropriate here since the judgment must be made as to whether or not the program goals are being met. The summative evaluation will also provide an asssessment of the values that are incorporated into the program. The initial presumption may have been that low reading comprehension and writing ability are hindrances to success in college. If the special program for low-ability students is successful, however, the initial value or presumption is altered. After the evaluation, one may presume that low verbal scores suggest that a student would benefit from the special program.

## MODELS AND DECISIONS

The first section of this chapter was intended to discuss evaluation and program planning using generally accepted notions about evaluation. This section is a summary of evaluation models or techniques in terms of the type of decisions to which they are addressed.

The way in which evaluation is conducted depends, to some extent, upon the type of decision one wants to make or the type of influence one wants to have as a result of the evaluation. The general strategy for conducting an evaluation is often referred to as a *model* of evaluation.

By far the most common evaluation model is the goal-based model. Goal-based evaluation is directed to answering the question, "Is the program accomplishing the goals it was intended to meet?" In the example above, the program designed to improve the rate of learning of students admitted with low verbal scores is a goal-directed program, and that program could be evaluated using a goal-based model of evaluation.

A second evaluation model is called the *descriptive evaluation* model. An example is *goal-free evaluation,* (Scriven, 1973). This model, like the first, is oriented towards the description of outcomes or products. In contrast to the goal-based model, the descriptive model or goal-free model ignores the intended goals of a program and focuses on a description of its actual outcomes. It is designed to answer the question, "What has this program accomplished?"

A third evaluation model can be described as a *decision-oriented* model or the program survival model (for example, see Stufflebeam, 1971). This model of evaluation assumes that the evaluation is conducted for the benefit of a specific audience of decision makers. Among other things, the decision makers will determine whether or not a particular program survives. The program survival model is designed to answer the question. "What information do the decision makers need in order to make a judgment about the success of the program?"

Colleges and universities have a history of functioning on a variation of the decision-oriented model, the *external criterion* model. With this model, the performance of a program or an individual is judged in terms of criteria established by an external agency or through expert judgment. Most institutional accreditations are based on an external criterion model. The review of manuscripts for publication, the grading of essay examinations, and the grading of term papers all employ this particular assessment model. One difficulty with the external criterion model is that the criteria for assessing goodness are often not specified to those whose performance is being evaluated. This creates two problems: first, it is difficult for those who are being evaluated to improve without clear knowledge of what is expected; and secondly, this model can result in a great deal of resistance to change because the criteria of goodness are subject to disagreement.

A recently developed model of evaluation that has created interest is referred to as *portrayal evaluation* or *responsive evaluation*. This model of evaluation attempts to reflect the entire breadth of a program, including its goal-directed activities and its broader impact on the milieu in which it operates. Parlett and Dearden (1977) describe a version of portrayal evaluation, illuminative evaluation, that has become particularly popular in higher education circles. Portrayal evaluation places as much emphasis on obtaining qualitative information as quantitative data. Further, the evaluator is in the position of interpreting a program rather than assuring that its results will be valuable.

Many of the models of evaluation are based on the accumulation of quantitative data. The design of evaluation studies and the development of assessment instruments or tests require technical sophistication. It is wise for a curriculum task force to locate a colleague or hire a consultant before embarking on an extensive evaluation project. Dressel (1976, Chapter 6) and Isaac and Michael (1972) are good sources as one begins to consider the issues and techniques that are most important in evaluating general education programs. The selection of professionally developed tests should also be done with care. Bess (1979) has listed a variety of student assessment instruments that are appropriate for measuring the outcomes of college and university instruction. Buros (1972) is considered an authoritative source who has extensively summarized data about educational and psychological instruments in a series of *Mental Measurement Yearbooks*.

Recently, several special projects have been initiated that focus on general education curricula and goals. Some of these have been designed to deal with the special problems associated with competency-based general education programs (see Pottinger, 1979; Wodisch, 1977). Models of this type of assessment are being used at Alverno College, Brigham Young University, and Mars Hill College, and sample materials are usually available through those institutions. These evaluations have been designed to certify that a student has met the minimum requirements in one area of the general education program at a particular institution.

Three other projects have been established to identify broader measures of student performance that could be standardized or employed in comparative studies. One of these is the College Outcome Measures Project (COMP) organized by the American College Testing Program (Forrest, 1979). This program developed instruments that measure the acquisition of knowledge and the application of generic skills in several areas of general or liberal education. The instruments employed in COMP have been field tested and are available for use. A similar study on Academic Competence in General Education has been undertaken through the Educational Testing Service (Warren, 1978) although the instruments employed in that program are not yet available for distribution. Field testing of measures of communication skills, analytic thinking, synthesizing ability, and cultural awareness is being done this year in a grouping of institutions in the American Association of State Colleges and Universities.

The third project, the Value Added Study at Harvard University, began with the assumption that earlier measurement attempts had provided only marginal results about the benefits of liberal education because the instruments were not appropriately designed to assess intellectual growth (Whitla, 1977). Using existing theoretical models, these researchers modified or developed eight instruments including two questionnaires. Comparisons were made across three types of institutions, private, state, and two-year, and between freshmen and students in the graduating class, either sophomores or seniors. While these instruments produced interesting results, they must be interpreted only as suggesting that a liberal arts education contributes to intellectual growth and maturity (Whitla, 1977; Winter, Stewart, and McClelland, 1978). Additional research is needed to sort out the various factors that contribute to that growth and maturity, such as various components of the general education program.

Two management instruments are available from the Educational Testing Service that could be used to provide background information during the initial stages of planning. They are the Institutional Functioning Inventory (IFI) and the Institutional Goals Inventory (IGI). The IGI can assist in clarifying the commitment of faculty, administrators, and students to various institutional goals, and the IFI can assist in identifying the effective and weak areas of institutional operation that would impinge upon the success of general education programs.

In summary, there seems to be no single model for effective evaluation. Indeed, several models may be useful, each containing several phases. Moreover, as this review illustrates, the literature for the most part includes only a few direct applications to the specific area of general education. The challenge is for curriculum designers and program evaluators to adapt what is known about evaluation from other contexts to design useful evaluations that parallel the establishment of new programs. In this way innovators can identify and correct early problems as well as demonstrate, to themselves as well as to outsiders, the value of their new programs of general education.

# ANNOTATED BIBLIOGRAPHY

Anderson, S. and Ball, S. *The Profession and Practice of Program Evaluation*. San Francisco: Jossey-Bass, 1978.
> The authors rely upon their experience to summarize the major models of program evaluation, and include insightful and practical examples. Part I surveys evaluation practices and is especially helpful. This discussion focusses on straight-forward techniques and the use of evidence in decision-making.

Bess, J. "Classroom and Management Decisions Using Student Data: Designing an Information System." *Journal of Higher Education*, May/June 1979, pp. 256-279.
> This article summarizes the decisions that are involved in selecting instruments and data that can be helpful in determining the effectiveness of classroom instruction. The traditional distinctions between student, content, and teaching are maintained. The article includes several practical examples and an extensive summary of instruments that are appropriate.

Dressel, P. *Handbook of Academic Evaluation*. San Francisco: Jossey-Bass, 1976.
> Based on considerable experience in higher education, the author surveys the major areas of evaluation in higher education. The first section is directed to a series of evaluation models, techniques, and attitudes. The second section covers practical areas, student recruitment, the learning environment, educational processes and teaching, examinations and evaluations in courses, and grading. The final section provides examples of evaluation applied to curricular decisions, personnel decisions, institutional self-study, and multi-institutional systems. The discussions are all laced with practical solutions to political problems and to overcoming resource difficulties. The author advocates an eclectic and flexible approach to evaluation.

Forrest, A, "Competence in the Effectively Functioning Citizen." In P. Pottinger and J. Goldsmith, eds. *New Directions for Experiential Learning: Defining and Measuring Competence*. San Francisco: Jossey-Bass, 1979, p. 85-93.
> The American College Testing Program's College Outcome Measures Project (COMP) is described. The author claims that knowledge and skills important to the effectively functioning adult can be measured by new instruments. The strengths and weakness of this approach are also summarized.

Genova, W., Madoff, M., Chin, R. and Thomas, G. *Mutual Benefit Evaluation of Faculty and Administrators in Higher Education*. Cambridge, Mass.: Ballinger, 1976.
> The authors have written a small but thorough guide to evaluation of educational staff. The assumption is that faculty, administrators, and students are brought together in a cybernetic system, and the benefits produced by each should enter the staff evaluation. The approach is practical, and the suggestions are clear. These ideas could be adapted easily to competence-based or outcome-based general education programs.

Grant, D., ed. *Monitoring Ongoing Programs*. San Francisco: Jossey-Bass, 1978.
> This volume includes both practical and theoretical articles about the maintenance of quality through program monitoring. Adaptable examples are included. The article on higher education highlights some of the difficulties in monitoring actual programs.

Grasha, A. *Assessing and Developing Faculty Performance: Principles and Models*. Cincinnati: Communication and Education Associates, 1977.
> This manual clearly develops a rationale for evaluation performance: faculty performance has an impact on students. The principles for classroom assessment and the suggestions for implementing faculty evaluation could easily be adapted to many general education program evaluation needs.

Hodgkinson, H., Hurst, J., and Levine, H. *Improving and Assessing Performance: Evaluation in Higher Education*. Berkeley, Calif.: Center for Research and Development in Higher Education, University of California, 1975.
> The authors assume that performance assessment is an essential element in improving the effectiveness of higher education programs. They muster a rationale to support that assumption and illustrate it by example.

Isaac, S. and Michael, W. *Handbook in Research and Evaluation.* San Diego: Robert R. Knapp, 1972.

This brief handbook includes a thorough set of guidelines for program evaluation. It also discusses most of the major technical issues associated with evaluation research. The examples are all appropriate for educational evaluation problems.

Katzenmeyer, C. *Evaluation: A Common Sense Approach.* Washington, D.C.: Association of American Colleges, 1979.

This author has written a straightforward discussion of practical issues and approaches to program evaluation. Although his intended audience is proposal writers, the issues and examples are appropriate for general education program planning. Includes useful suggestions about the selection of consultants.

King, S. "Assessment of Competence: Technical Problems and Publications" In G. Grant, et al., eds. *On Competence.* San Francisco: Jossey-Bass, 1979, pp. 491-520.

The assessment of competence and the certification of competence are briefly described in this chapter. Several models of assessment that are appropriate for competence-based programs are summarized. An annotated bibliography of competence and assessment sources is included.

Knapp, J. and Sharon, A. *Compendium of Assessment Techniques.* Princeton, N.J.: Educational Testing Service, 1974.

A variety of assessment techniques is summarized, and an extensive reference list is included. The assessment techniques cover the range from those appropriate for traditional programs to those that can be applied in the assessment of learning by experience.

Miller, R. *Developing Programs for Faculty Evaluation: A Sourcebook for Higher Education.* San Francisco: Jossey-Bass, 1974.

This text is useful in two respects. First, it illustrates the relationship between a planned evaluation and the usefulness of an evaluation in effecting future change. Second, it summarizes criteria that can be used to assess teaching and advising, and it provides a thoughtful discussion of student ratings as a source of data for teaching evaluation. Sample case studies of teacher and administrator evaluations are included along with annotated reference lists.

Milton, O. & Associates. *On College Teaching.* San Francisco: Jossey-Bass, 1978.

The authors summarize the teaching techniques most frequently used in higher education. Each is reviewed in terms of the evaluation research about it, and suggestions are made about steps that could be taken to improve each technique. From the perspective of program evaluation, these summaries are useful in suggesting factors that might be assessed when a program evaluation is being conducted. The chapter on classroom testing also provides useful suggestions to improve instructor-made tests.

Milton, O. and Edgerly, J. *The Testing and Grading of Students.* New Rochelle, N.Y.: Change Magazine Press, 1976.

Practical discussions of the issues involved in testing students and in the construction of tests are included. The relationship between assessment and evaluation of students is carefully and thoroughly explored. The authors list annotated references.

Pace, C. *Measuring Outcomes of College.* San Francisco: Jossey-Bass, 1979.

This book summarizes 50 years of testing the achievement of undergraduates, many studies of college alumni, as well as self- and comparative studies of colleges. In addition to synthesizing what has been learned about undergraduate accomplishment, the author offers ideas about how to improve the measures of evaluation.

Suchman, E. *Evaluative Research: Principles and Practice in Public Service and Social Action Programs.* New York: Russell Sage Foundation, 1967.

This is one of the classics in the area of program evaluation. Suchman develops a rationale for evaluation, shows how to plan an evaluation and how to conduct it, and suggests the strengths and weaknesses of different evaluation models.

Whitla, D. *Value Added: Measuring the Outcomes of Undergraduate Education.* Unpublished manuscript available from Dean K. Whitla, Office of Instructional Research and Evaluation, Harvard University, Cambridge, Mass. 02138, 1977.

This report summarizes the rationale behind the Harvard Value Added study and the results of that study. The results on each of the eight measures of student performance are intepreted for each student sample. The student samples are drawn from three types of institutions—two-year, four-year public, and four-year private.

Winter, D., Stewart, A. and McClelland, D. "Grading the Effects of a Liberal Arts Education." *Psychology Today*, September, 1978, pp. 69-74.
Another summary of a portion of the results of the Value Added study. This report focusses on the measures derived from the Test of Thematic Apperception. The authors interpret the results as supporting the hypothesis that a liberal arts education does improve one's thinking.

## ADDITIONAL BIBLIOGRAPHY

Airasian, P. "Designing Summative Evaluation Studies at the Local Level." In W. Popham, ed., *Evaluation in Education*. Berkeley, Calif.: McCutchan, 1974, pp. 147-99.

Alverno College Faculty. *Assessment at Alverno*. Milwaukee, Wis.: Alverno College, 1979.

Anderson, S., Ball, S., Murphy, R. *Encyclopedia of Educational Evaluation: Concepts and Techniques for Evaluating Education and Training Programs*. San Francisco: Jossey-Bass, 1974.

Baker, E. and Popham, W. *Expanding Dimensions of Instructional Objectives*. Englewood Cliffs, N.J.: Prentice-Hall, 1973.

Bloom, B., ed. *Taxonomy of Educational Objectives: The Classification of Educational Goals—Handbook 1. Cognitive Domain*. New York: McKay, 1956.

Bloom, B., Hastings, J., and Madaus, G. *Handbook on Formative and Summative Evaluation of Student Learning*. New York: McGraw-Hill, 1971.

Borich, G., ed. *Evaluating Educational Programs and Products*. Englewood Cliffs, N.J.: Educational Technology Publications, 1974.

Bowen, H. and Douglass, G. *Efficiency in Liberal Education*. New York: McGraw-Hill, 1971.

Buros, O., ed. *The Seventh Mental Measurements Yearbook* 2. Highland Park, N.J.: Gryphon Press, 1972.

Carver, R. "Special Problems in Measuring Change with Psychometric Devices." In *Evaluative Research, Strategies, and Methods*. Pittsburgh: American Institutes for Research, 1970, pp. 18-35.

Carver, R. "Two Dimensions of Tests: Psychometric and Edumetric." *American Psychologist* 29, 1974, pp. 512-18.

Centra, J. *Determining Faculty Effectiveness*. San Francisco: Jossey-Bass, 1979.

Centra, J. *Colleagues as Raters of Classroom Instruction*. (Research Bulletin RB-74-18) Princeton: Educational Testing Service, 1974.

Centra, J. *The Relationship between Student and Alumni Ratings of Teachers*. )Research Bulletin RB-73-39) Princeton: Educational Testing Service, 1973.

Centra, J. *The Student as Godfather? The Impact of Student Ratings on Academic*. (Research Memorandum RM-73-8) Princeton: Educational Testing Service, 1973.

Charters, W. and Jones, J. "On the Risk of Appraising Non-Events in Program Evaluation." *Educational Researcher*, 2, No. 11, 1973, pp. 5-7.

Colteway, D. "An Evaluation of the Effect of Instructional Systems." Paper presented at the American Education Research Association Meeting, San Francisco, April, 1979. Available from author at Athabasca University, 14515-122 Avenue, Edmonton, Alberta, Canada 7662W4.

Cook, T. and Campbell, D. *Quasi-Experimentation: Design and Analysis Issues for Field Settings*. Chicago: Rand McNally College Publishing Company, 1979.

Cooley, W. "Assessment of Educational Effects." *Educational Psychologist,* 11, No. 1, 1974, pp. 29-35.

Cooley, W. and Lohnes, P. *Evaluation Research in Education*. New York: Irvington Publishers, Inc., 1976.

Cronbach, L. "Course Improvement through Evaluation." *Teacher's College Record* 64, 1963, pp. 672-83.

Cronbach, L. and Furby, L. "How Should We Measure 'Change'—or Should We?" *Psychological Bulletin* 74, 1970, pp. 68-80.

Doi, J., ed. "Assessing Faculty Effort." *New Directions for Higher Education*. San Francisco: Jossey-Bass, 1974.

Doyle, K., Jr. *Student Evaluation of Instruction*. Lexington, Ma.: D.C. Heath, 1975.

Dressel, P. *Handbook of Academic Evaluation*. San Francisco: Jossey-Bass, 1976.

Dressel, P. and Associates. *Institutional Research in Higher Education*. Boston: Houghton Mifflin, 1961.

Ebel, R. *Essentials in Educational Measurement*. Englewood Cliffs, N.J.: Prentice-Hall, 1972.

Eisner, E. "Educational Connoisseurship and Criticism: Their Form and Function in Educational Evaluation." *Journal of Aesthetic Education* 10, 1976, pp. 135-50.

Fear, R. *The Evaluation Interview*. (2d ed.) New York: McGraw-Hill, 1973.

Gaff, S., Festa, C., and Gaff, J. *Professional Development: A Guide to Resources*. New Rochelle, N.Y.: Change Magazine Press, 1978.

Grant, G. and Kohli, W. "Contributing to Learning by Assessing Student Performance." In G. Grant, et al., eds., *On Competence*. San Francisco: Jossey-Bass, 1979, pp. 138-59.

Haller, E. "Cost Analysis for Educational Program Evaluation." In W. Popham, ed., *Evaluation in Higher Education*. Berkeley, Calif.: McKutchan, 1974, pp. 399-450.

*A Handbook for Self-Assessment*. Self-Assessment for Colleges and Universities, Donald Tritschler, Project Director, Room 5A47, Cultural Education Center, New York State Education Department, Albany, New York, 12230.

Hodgkinson, H., Hurst, J., Levine, H., and Brint, S. *A Manual for the Evaluation of Innovative Programs and Practices in Higher Education*. Berkeley: Center for Research and Development in Higher Education, University of California, 1974.

House, E. *The Logic of Evaluative Argument*. CSE Monograph Series in Evaluations No. 7. Center for the Study of Evaluation, University of California, Los Angeles, 1977.

Hoyt, D. "College Grades and Adult Accomplishment." *Educational Record* 47, 1966, pp. 70-75.

Johnson, C. and Katzenmeyer, W., eds. *Management Information Systems in Higher Education: The State of the Art*. Durham, North Carolina: Duke University Press, 1969.

Katzenmeyer, G. "Evaluation: A Common Sense Approach." *Special Report, Federal Resources Advisory Service*. Washington, D.C.: Association of American Colleges, February, 1979.

Knapp, J. and Hamilton, I. *The Effect of Non-Standard Undergraduate Assessment and Reporting Practices on Graduate School Admissions Processes*. Princeton: Educational Testing Service, 1978.

Krathwohl, D., Bloom, B., and Masia, B. *Taxonomy of Educational Objectives: The Classification of Educational Goals—Handbook 2. Affective Domain*. New York: McKay, 1964.

Lenning, O. *The "Benefits Crisis" in Higher Education* (Report 1). Washington, D.C.: American Association for Higher Education, 1974.

Lenning, O. and Associates. *The Many Faces of College Success and Their Non-Intellective Correlates: The Published Literature*. Iowa City, Iowa: American College Testing Program, 1975.

Lessinger, L. "A Historical Note on Accountability in Education." *Journal of Research and Development in Education* 5, 1971, pp. 15-18.

Levin, H. "Cost Effectiveness Analysis in Evaluation Research." In M. Guttentog, ed., *Handbook of Evaluation Research*. Beverly Hills, Calif.: Sage Publications, 1975.

McKeachie, W., Lin, Y., and Mann, W. "Student Ratings of Teacher Effectiveness: Validity Studies." *American Educational Research Journal*, May, 1971, pp. 435-45.

Miller, R. *Evaluating Faculty Performance*. San Francisco: Jossey-Bass, 1972.

Miller, R. *The Assessment of College Performance*. San Francisco: Jossey-Bass, 1979.

Mishler, E. "Meaning in Context: Is There Any Other Kind?" *Harvard Educational Review*, February, 1979, pp. 1-19.

Najder, Z. *Values and Evaluation*. Oxford: Clarendon Press, 1975.

North, J. and Scholl, S. *Revising a Faculty Evaluation System*. Washington, D.C.: Small College Consortium, 1978.

O'Connell, W., Jr. and Meeth, R. *Evaluating Teaching Improvement Programs*. New Rochelle, N.Y.: Change Magazine Press, 1978.

Oppenheim, A. *Questionnaire Design and Attitude Design and Attitude Measurement*. New York: Basic Books, 1966.

Parlett, M. and Deardon, G. *Introduction to Illuminative Evaluation Studies in Higher Education*. Washington, D.C.: Council for the Advancement of Small Colleges, 1977.

Peterson, R., Centra, J., Hartnett, R., and Linn, R. *Institutional Functioning Inventory*. Princeton, N.J.: Educational Testing Service, 1970.

Popham, W., ed. *Evaluation in Education*. Berkeley, Calif.: McCutchan, 1974.

Pottinger, P. "Competence Assessment: Comments on Current Practices." In P. Pottinger and J. Goldsmith, eds., *Defining and Measuring Competence*. San Francisco: Jossey-Bass, 1979, pp. 25-40.

"Research Scientists Devise Ways to Assess Intellectual Growth." *ETS Development*. Princeton: Educational Testing Service, Winter, 1978.

Roueche, J. and Herrscher, B. *Toward Instructional Accountability: A Practical Guide to Educational Change*. Sunnyvale, Calif.: Westinghouse Learning Press, 1973.

Sanders, J. and Nafziger, D. *A Basis for Determining the Adequacy of Evaluation Designs*. Occasional Paper No. 6, Evaluation Center, College of Education, Western Michigan University, Kalamazoo, Michigan 49008, 1976.

Scriven, M. "Goal-Free Evaluation." In E. House, ed., *School Evaluation: The Politics and Process*. Berkeley, Calif.: McCutchan, 1973, pp. 24-42.

Scriven, M. "The Methodology of Evaluation." In *Perspectives of Curriculum Evaluation*, AERA Monograph Series on Curriculum Evaluation, No. 1. Chicago: Rand McNally, 1967, pp. 39-83.

Scriven, M. and Roth, J. "Needs Assessment: Concept and Practices." In S. Anderson and C. Coles, *New Directions for Program Evaluation: Exploring Purposes and Dimensions*. San Francisco: Jossey-Bass, 1978, 1-12.

Smith, P. "On the Logic of Behavioral Objectives." *Phi Delta Kappa*, March, 1972, pp. 429-430.

Smock, H. and Brandenburg, D. "Student Evaluation of Academic Programs." *Journal of Higher Education*, September/October, 1978, pp. 489-503.

Smock, H. and Crooks, T. "A Plan for the Comprehensive Evaluation of College Teaching." *Journal of Higher Education* 44, 1973, pp. 577-86.

Stake, R. "The Countenance of Educational Evaluation." *Teacher's College Record* 68, 1967, pp. 523-40.

Stake, R., ed. *Evaluating the Arts in Education: A Responsive Approach*. Columbus, Ohio: Charles E. Merrill, 1975.

Stake, R., ed. "Responsive Evaluation." In D. Hamilton, et.al., *Beyond the Numbers Game: A Reader in Educational Evaluation*. London: MacMillan, 1976, pp. 77-106.

Stone, J. "e-Value-ation." In S. Anderson and C. Coles, eds., *New Directions for Program Evaluation: Exploring Purposes and Dimensions*. San Francisco: Jossey-Bass, 1978, pp. 73-82.

Stufflebeam, D. "The Use of Experimental Design in Educational Evaluation." *Journal of Educational Measurement* 8, 1971, pp. 267-74.

Stufflebeam, D. and Associates. *Educational Evaluation and Decision Making*. Itasca, Illinois: Peacock, 1971.

Taylor, P. *Normative Discourse*. Englewood Cliffs, N.J.: Prentice-Hall, 1961.

Trow, M. "Methodological Problems in the Evaluation of Innovation." In M. Wittrock and D. Wiley, eds., *The Evaluation of Instruction: Issues and Problems*. New York: Holt, Rinehart & Winston, 1970, pp. 289-305.

Tyler, R. *Basic Principles of Curriculum and Instruction*. Chicago: University of Chicago Press, 1950.

Tyler, R. "The Functions of Measurement in Improving Instruction." In E. Lindquist, ed., *Educational Measurement*. Washington, D.C.: American Council on Education, 1951, pp. 12-16.

Tyler, R. "Tests as a Means of Measuring Educational Programs, Methods, and Instructional Materials." In R. Tyler and R. Wolf, eds., *Crucial Issues in Testing*. Berkeley, Calif.: McCutchan, 1974, pp. 143-55.

Van Maanen, J. "The Process of Program Evaluation." *Grantsmanship Center News*, January/February, 1979, pp. 30-74. The Grantsmanship Center, 917 15th St., N.W., Washington, D.C. 20003.

Warren, J. *The Measurement of Academic Competence*. Berkeley, Calif.: Educational Testing Service, 1978. Unpublished paper available from J. Warren, Educational Testing Service, 1947 Center St., Berkeley, Calif., 94704.

Webb, E. and Associates. *Unobtrusive Measures: Nonreactive Research in the Social Sciences*. Chicago: Rand McNally, 1966.

Whitla, D. *Value Added: Measuring the Outcomes of Undergraduate Education*. Office of Instructional Research and Evaluation, Harvard University, Cambridge, Ma. 02138, 1977.

Willis, G., ed. *Qualitative Evaluation: Concepts and Cases in Curriculum Criticism*. Berkeley, Calif.: McCutchan, 1978.

Winstead, P. *Systematic Institutional Planning: Furman's Approach.* Paper presented at the Eleventh Annual Conference of the Society for College and University Planning, July, 1976. Available from author at Furman University, Greenville, South Carolina, 29613.

Winter, D. *Defining and Measuring the Competencies of a Liberal Arts Education.* Paper presented at the National Conference on Higher Education, sponsored by the American Association for Higher Education, April, 1979.

Winter, D., Stewart, A., and McClelland, D. "Grading the Effects of a Liberal Arts Education." *Psychology Today,* September 1978, pp. 69-75.

Wittrock, M. and Wiley, D., eds. *The Evaluation of Instruction: Issues and Problems.* New York: Holt, Rinehart & Winston, 1970.

Woditsch, G. *Developing Generic Skills: A Model for Competency Based Education.* Bowling Green, Ohio: CUE Project (Bowling Green State University), 1977.

Worthen, B. and Sanders, J., eds. *Educational Evaluation: Theory and Practice.* Worthington, Ohio: Jones, 1973.

## PROGRAMS FOR EVALUATION

American College Testing Program
The College Outcome Measures Project
2201 North Dodge Street
P.O. Box 168
Iowa City, Iowa 52240
Aubrey Forrest, Director, Instruction Design and Assessment

The College Outcomes Measures Project has designed three assessment instruments to measure the knowledge and skills that undergraduate students are expected to acquire as a result of general and liberal education programs. The Measurement Battery involves a series of materials, activities, and questions requiring students to provide their own answers. The Objective Test is a machine-scored proxy for the Measurement Battery. The Activity Inventory asks students about the quantity and quality of their participation in adult roles in college as predictors of their future levels of performance.

Alverno College
Milwaukee, Wisconsin 53215
Austin Doherty, Vice President for Academic Affairs

Alverno was one of the first institutions to transform its curriculum to a competence-based program. The development of several competencies, and of alternative means of teaching them, plus the skill required by the faculty to evaluate their outcomes have all been important steps in curriculum revision at Alverno. Some of the areas of competence are "analytical capability," "valuing in a decision making context," "effectiveness in individual environment," "responsible involvement in the contemporary world," and "esthetic responsiveness." The advanced specialized levels are developed as necessary for the student's area of concentration and support areas. Faculty orient their teaching toward integrating discipline and competence areas.

Council for the Advancement of Experiential Learning
Fifty College Project
American City Building, Suite 208
Columbia, Maryland 21044
Morris Keeton, Executive Director

The project focuses on training faculty and equipping them with aids to the mapping of intended learning outcomes and the prerequisites to students' achieving those outcomes. In keeping with CAEL's emphasis upon the values of experiential learning, special emphasis is given to the learning outcomes best developed in off-campus experiences. The project is producing a set of workbooks usable by both students and faculty members in planning courses of study.

Educational Testing Service
1947 Center Street
Berkeley, California 94704
Jonathan R. Warren, Research Psychologist

With the Support of the Fund for the Improvement of Postsecondary Education, the ETS has conducted a research project to assess student achievement in four areas associated with general education: communication skills, analytic thinking, synthesizing ability, and cultural awareness. Questions, procedures, and instruments for assessing programmatic effectiveness in general education in each of these areas have been developed. These materials are currently being field tested in a project of the Resource Center for Planned Change of the American Association of State Colleges and Universities.

McBer and Company
Comprehensive Cognitive Assessment Battery
137 Newberry Street
Boston, Massachusetts 02116
Howard H. Russell, Program Manager

The Comprehensive Cognitive Assessment Battery is the result of a study of educational outcomes. The tests create actual tasks or situations that are similar to the educational process and/or real life, and then ask subjects to develop responses. Four tests comprise the Battery: the Test of Thematic Analysis, a measure of critical thinking ability; Analysis of Argument, a measure of intellectual flexibility; Learning Style Inventory, a measure of perceived learning style; and Test of Self-Definition, a measure of whether a person habitually thinks in terms of causes and outcomes.

Mars Hill College
Mars Hill, North Carolina 28754
David Knisley, Associate Academic Dean

The general education curriculum at Mars Hill College is organized around six ways of knowing: Symbolic Communications, Personal Knowledge, Aesthetics, Valuing, Science, and Synoptics. For each of these ways of knowing, a competence has been specified which students must demonstrate before graduation. Especially designed courses enable students to attain the specified competences, but students may also attain them in independent study, internships, life and work experience, or any other way they choose. Students may demonstrate their competence in a variety of ways including successful completion of designated courses, CLEP, and Advanced Placement examinations, locally developed competence examinations, and assessment team juries. Entering students are tested to ascertain their abilities and course placement in written communication, foreign language, reading, and mathematics. A similar program in science is under development.

National Center for Higher Education Management Systems
The Outcomes Structure
P. O. Box P
Boulder, Colorado 80302
Ben Lawrence, Executive Director

The Outcomes Structure was designed to help people on campuses think in systematic, concrete, and specific terms about student outcomes of educational programs. Many educators are accustomed to thinking about activities without conspicuously addressing the goals or results of those tasks. By using a special questionnaire, faculty, students, and administrators can identify needs and goals and agree upon priorities for them. The process can be modified for targets as small as students majoring in a single department or as wide as state systems.

Western Michigan University
The Evaluation Center
Kalamazoo, Michigan 49008
Daniel L. Stufflebeam, Director

To advance the science and practice of evaluation, the Center provides research, development, instruction, dissemination, and service. Over the past ten years, the Center has worked in these areas with local school districts, state departments of education, foundations, and federal agencies. Although little work has been specifically in general education, the Center has studied the effects of school-based evaluation offices on school practice, evaluation theory, and techniques for meeting special evaluation objectives.

University of California, Los Angeles
Laboratory for Research on Higher Education
405 Hilgard Avenue
Los Angeles, California 90024
C. Robert Pace, Director

The Laboratory is an interdisciplinary center for research, evaluation, information, and policy studies in higher education. Among the projects of the Laboratory is the Higher Education Measurement and Evaluation kit, which contains sample formats and questions for measuring student progress and attainment, educational processes, and characteristics of the student body.